Parvit of Agelast

for the small

PARVIT OF AGELAST

A Fantasy in Verse

Máighréad Medbh

PARVIT OF AGELAST

is published in 2016 by
ARLEN HOUSE
42 Grange Abbey Road
Baldoyle
Dublin 13
Ireland
Phone/Fax: 353 86 8207617
Email: arlenhouse@gmail.com

Distributed internationally by
SYRACUSE UNIVERSITY PRESS
621 Skytop Road, Suite 110
Syracuse, NY 13244–5290
Phone: 315–443–5534/Fax: 315–443–5545
Email: supress@syr.edu

ISBN 978–1–85132–158–2, paperback

Typesetting ¦ Arlen House

Cover image by Pauline Bewick
'Eggshell Woman, Slate Man'
2003 • eggshell, slate dust, acrylic & goldleaf • 42″ x 57″
reproduced with the kind permission of the artist

CONTENTS

Author's Note

It started as a desire to 'escape', to be apolitical, amoral, irresponsible. I wrote a poem called 'Yellow Woman', a dialogue between a 'seeker' and a woman who lives somewhere within wild vegetation. Soon after, I recognised a similar woman in several paintings by Pauline Bewick. We met and I spent time looking closely at her work.

What I originally conceived as an ekphrastic sequence of about twenty poems morphed into an examination of fear, imprisonment and liberty, and then became a scenario with a story to tell. It's an allegory, though I largely let the events go their own way, and the mode is impressionistic.

While a few of Pauline's paintings appear as themselves, her *Eggshell Woman, Slate Man* was the main visual catalyst. The rest I constructed as if I were writing a fantasy novel, with its own inherent logic.

Agelast is a slate city, geometrically planned, with a sacred pyramid at its centre. The prevailing belief, inculcated by the oligarchic government, is that there's nothing beyond the city wall, and no way of reaching or penetrating the white cloud-cover that squares everything off. All essential products are mined from the ground, food is in the form of pills, desire of all kinds is kept subdued. The ground is thought of as male and the sky female; Sky, Ground and City constitute one self-generated god.

Parvit begins as a lump of matter hidden in the city wall, unwilling to be a conscious participant in anything, afraid to take a shape, but she's experiencing more than she realises. She's a conduit to the world we recognise as reality, where she encounters various fear-inducing situations of imprisonment, and their counterpoints in escapist ecstasy.

The watching giants were an instinctual addition. They complete the picture, which is somewhat cinematic and often surreal.

Acknowledgements

The pivotal visual metaphors are Pauline Bewick's grey/yellow opposition and the painting, *Eggshell Woman, Slate Man.* The following poems are responses to particular paintings: 'Woman and Frog'; 'Dancing Girl, Kenmare' and 'Dream of an Odd Career' (*Woman, Water and Oak Tree*). I'm very grateful to Pauline for her hospitality, her generosity in talking to me about her work, the use of her image, and her continued support.

The city grew from my own images and concepts. Any resemblance to the philosophies, motifs and symbols of religious and other organisations is accidental.

The quotations used are from the following sources:

'Pine': Jaycee Dugard, *A Stolen Life* (London, Simon & Schuster, 2011), p. 62.

'Laredo': Joaquín Guzmán Loera, http://en.wikipedia.org/wiki/2012_Nuevo_Laredo_massacres

'Little Queen': Malika Oufkir, *Freedom: The Story of My Second Life* (New York, Hyperion, 2006), p. 228.

'Smalled': Natascha Kampusch, *3,096 Days*, trans. Jill Kreuer (London, Penguin, 2010), p. 121.

'Cut': Waris Dirie, *Desert Children* (London, Virago, 2005), p. 9.

'net': Ciara Pugsley, online conversation: http://ask.fm/likes/pugsley/question/748342596/mobile_prompt

'Seized': Laurie Halse Anderson, http://www.goodreads.com/quotes/tag/rape

'Witness': Zia Awan, http://www.theguardian.com/world/2014/may/27/pregnant-pakistani-woman-stoned-to-death

'Woman and Frog': Pauline Bewick, conversation, commenting on the painting.

'Hide': Eva Kor, http://www.sciencedaily.com/releases/2012/12/121206153357.htm

'Another Dimension': Tamara de Lempicka, quoted in Laura Claridge, *Tamara de Lempicka* (London, Bloomsbury, 1999), p. 33.

'Dancing Girl, Kenmare': Pauline Bewick, *Pauline Bewick's Seven Ages,* Alan Hayes ed. (Galway, Arlen House, 2006).

'Devil's Wine': Lyn Madden and June Levine, *Lyn: A Story of Prostitution* (Cork, Attic Press, 2004), p. 267.

'mammy long legs': Jaycee Dugard, *A Stolen Life* (London, Simon & Schuster, 2011), p. 66.

'Proof of Life': Ingrid Betancourt, *Even Silence Has an End,* (London, Virago, 2010), p. 495.

'Three Good Reasons to be a Vivienne Westwood Tartan Dress': Vivienne Westwood, http://fashion.telegraph.co.uk/news-features/TMG8691362/Vivienne-Westwoods-mission-to-save-the-world-one-handbag-at-a-time.html

'Virgin by Desire': Web MD, http://www.webmd.com/women/picture-of-the-vagina

'post': David Bentley (Marriage Counsellor),

http://denver-marriage-counseling.com/2011/03/understanding-men/

'Breatharian': Joachim M. Werdin, *Life Style Without Food,* p. 51. Online at http://www.librarising.com/health/lswf.pdf

'The Key to Paradise': Adel Sadew, Head of Department of Psychiatry at Cairo University, quoted in *Army of Roses* by Barbara Victor (London, Constable and Robinson, 2004), p. 26.

'Gone': Frida Kahlo, http://thinkexist.com/quotes/frida_kahlo/

'In the beginning was the closed eye, and so it will be in the end. In here happens all that will happen. In here all things are made that are made'.

– from *The Lore of the Ancestors*

'There is time', says Giant to Daughter. 'You can stop and look'.

'But there are so many places, and so much to be done', says Daughter, wild with her endless compulsions.

'There is time', Giant says, sucking a Daughter-eye from its matrix and placing it at the centre of a hollow cube within her own incalculable mass.

The walls of the cube are black at first, then become silver screens. The eye understands that there is about to be a show, but an eye does not decipher, only relays.

Agelast

AERIAL APPROACH

White, slush thick, silver glints, green spots, a red tint.
Traces of ore and settled gold, dints of crystalline spikes.
Slumps of gray, streal of icy droplets, flinty sleet hails.
But a unitary feel. A halted, vast, conspiratorial mash.

No instrument can pilot through, no pilot attempts.
It's a stomach, a full bowl. Stake your fork and cling.
Nothing pulls. Opposites collapse. Undescription.
History spread so thin it covers everything.

Challenge. Frustration. You sigh and go under. Should
you sleep, ruminate, or shovel to sheds the drippings,
the million blunted swords? You forget grass,
mountain, open sky, all that's radical in rock,

resign to hope. Miss the sudden scatter, that instant
when you first view Agelast, city of slate, designing
your fall to its order, tonguing you to its hard core.
Dense white cloud above; below, four-square gloam.

Zooming In

Square city of radiating streets, within high walls.
What impresses most is the porcupine of spires.
They bristle and watch, you swear it, fending spurs
on a square wheel, the hub a raised pyramid
black as a dormant volcano with a dunce's cap.

Soon you are level with the top of a building, look in
to a lighted office, a low-sized, brawny man circuiting
the long windows, mic to mouth, officials at screens.
Then scud through an untransected street of giddy-
tall towers, free-standing, at measured intervals.

The sound of heaving makes you turn and think
the scene behind contracts and settles, breathing out.
Ahead, the street questions you and the towers seem to
pull back, like lonely men at the touch of a woman.
Continue straight as a javelin, full-stop at the wall.

No way now but back – to the city's core, the Krone.

Omphalos

The Krone is half the height of a tower,
but it duplicates, inverted, underneath.
The citizens think it self-illumined, inlit
by transfusion from veins of buried ore.

Its green-and-silver sheen is not an invitation,
except for priests, officials, prisoners and the dead.
They say the stone is hot as an oven, so pilgrims
kneel on the bottom step and extend their palms.

It is where all directions begin. From Funeral Gate
to the city wall is lower Agelast, right and left.
Procession Gate faces upper city and Access Gate
is on the centre line. All travel orients from its points.

The pyramid is totem and powerhouse, prime edifice.
Its priests mine for inspiration, cremate and sacrifice.
Ashes of the dead go to Ground, their smoke to Sky
(but the eye in the Skyward apex is mostly shut).

Data

Distance is in urgons. Agelast is 16 urgons squared.
The urgon is a ratio of effort to gain, converted.
16,000 urges in an urgon, subdivided to micros.
There is no zero. Count from 1, within the fixed walls.

The 4 sectors, equal in size, are defined by social type:
Alpha, Theta, Beta, Gamma – clockwise.
Travel is only for commerce. You reside where born.
Daily traffic rounds the Krone, and later returns.

Residents of Alpha are the Null, menial workers.
Opposite, the Deft of Beta: expert in science and craft.
In Gamma, the Stern make laws, run banks and mines,
while Theta's Glib are masters of fashion and games.

4 thick walls border the sectors, cruciform, lower
than the city wall, measured multiples of a man.
The towers are lower still, but each 81 storeys high,
256 of them, ecosystematically designed.

GENESIS
(from *The Lore of the Ancestors*)

'A solitary stone is a weak one, prone to obsolescence.
And so the Great Crush decreed unity, amalgamation.
Annexed by the march of empire, one tastes the breadth
of immortality. Little feeds large; morpheme to lexicon.
Pulverised shale is restored in a crystal resurrection.
Behold: the elevation of quartz; the golding of pyrite;
the diaspora of silicates; mica's foiled rebellion
reforged in the indurated logic of the new state. Agelast
was formed of this unitary spirit, slow in a closed fire.
Its elements endure in the towers and streets, pumping
history through every captive stroke. Hear the gray choir
in utter harmony, each tone pure, discrete, interleaving.
Citizens are offspring, not architects, risen like sparks.
The same close breath, now hot, now cold, transfigured
shale to slate, slate to city, city to its seed and stock.
Agelast, self-conceiving, is its own immanent god'.

pitiless, and the steely white, always white Sky
(Sky not always steely, sometimes gauzy,
mostly dull and with the tone of faded cloth).
falls like missiles on the equally metallic streets.
equally matched. a fervid battle starts,
slate battling slam, a pummelling of noise.
children peer from windows, shrunken silent,
pinched and polished faces in their gray hoods.
clap their hands when in a water-charming dance
here come the Deft, weaving through the maelstrom,
mystics in a hail of spears. you see them start
but in a pulse they're shadows in the liquid veil,
and it's a game to trace them through the rabid air
so far along the street as necks can reach.
Deft are quicker than the rain, and tougher;
we will gather, sing the progeny of Agelast.

Propitiation

The man of business and the child have the impulse
to emerge and stake their claim upon the streets,
gasping after the deluge. The water sluices to tanks,
processors whirr into action, and in gratitude,
all advance down the sixteen routes to the Krone.

There are no cars on the sacred Circus, where sixteen
orbital lanes hold the crush of worshippers, palms
towards the pyramid over the cordon of police
and four haloes of steps. Krone begins a low hum
the crowd echoes. Priests emerge in two solemn lines,

flanking the hierarch with the Shrine of the Pyramid.
Behold the eternal protolith, monotheme unmoulded.
The Krone-song is silver, then red, then crystal blue,
travels up bloodstreams and reminds them that if rain
has come, the air will soon be shot with gelben spikes

(a heat that only one phosphorescent being can abide).

Parvit

No-one knows the passage in the wall at Burobaile.
It's a slice of unsuspected habitation, sheltering
Parvit, asleep on her hard bed, soft that she is.

Malleable that she is, her body like pockless dough.
No eyes, but vivid images received, signals converted
by an inner light to show her how the world moves.

Where she lies, lodged within the fissured rock,
unrisen Parvit, what could be face is lower
than what must be feet, so all the city slides distorted

into her slant: long twisted towers, limp spires,
streets askew, potted plants bulbing at her rim,
faces in their daily fervours (His face, her nemesis).

Volts of rem experience make her undulate –
horrid beetles under the skin – but deep delta
spreadings underwrite her and, safely defused,
she in her sealike stance learns all she can hold.

Daughter-eye giants itself.

'She's a worm in the fruit', Daughter-Giant says, and waits for Giant's answer. When there is only silence, she opines to herself, 'She's too soft to be the seed'.

She ruminates.

'Strange how an eye connects to mind and mind still doesn't get the picture. I know of no city like this, but I've heard of the plans of great architects in the face of pollution'.

She coughs. She coughs louder and waits for her mother to shower her with blessings. Nothing comes. Sleeping, she presumes, and takes a long, deep breath. Might as well let Daughter-eye show her some more.

Parvit Dreams of Unhappy Shes

Parvit Being Slug

Wet enough, and always dusk, but Slug demurs
and tightens to perself. Foetally.
The long foot beneath per skirt on per ventral
side is an ergonomic stroke of genius
in His dark design (*Yes*, per hears, *Mine*).

Per stirs in hope to use per bonelessness
in peristaltic grace to flee Him, but
maybe Slug's a turd. Hermaphroditic
badness makes per situation static. Per eludes
the hard facts only slid between the slate sheets.

Slug is unalike, Law non-applicable, His
paragraphs declined. Lungless, eyeless (per thinks),
no clitoris to speak of agitation, feelers re-
tractable, plus smell. But within per livelong
laving and circular trail-tracing, Slug on occasion
finds the seed of a tall pine.

Pine

'Sleep is the only escape I have. When I don't dare think, I dare to dream'
– Jaycee Dugard

Each autumn, in Lake Tahoe, El Dorado county, CA,
the kokanee salmon turn from silver-blue to vermilion.
They spawn and die, their carcasses meat for mink

that unabused women sport as symbols of some love.
The kokanee is only native since 1944, so a mere child
to the happy-birthday lake two million years old.

Jaycee's eleven were a tiny tint to that time spread,
the moment when her fingers touched the pine cone –
print to Fibonacci imprint – a netsuke eye;

that darkened in the small backyard shed where sleep
was the better act, and a gnarled man made her desire
the woody grenade, her last memory of the outside.

A pine can last a thousand years; Jaycee eighteen, held
in the pulp of a small brain, twisted in, never knowing
what would sprout when a forest fire melted the resin
and out fell, in hazardous liberation, winged seeds.

Nuevo Laredo

'... all dead in Nuevo Laredo are pure scums'
– Joaquín Guzmán Loera/El Chapo

No-one knows rightly the source of the name, *Laredo*.
In a city incarnate of memory, where was it lost?

La policia brakes at the warehouse, balks at the screech.
Everything's hot and electric. *Plato o plomo.*

Projecting a liminal walkway fends off their eyes.
Her hip is as naked as midnight. *Mama es tan valiente.*

The gangster's taut little, tough little body is fractal.
Abdomen, head and thorax all modelled the same.

Her colleagues are cowed to a circle, attempt a cocoon.
But old shells are thicker than new, by the strut of him,

pace of him, scutty dictator. She reaches for hate; acid
is all she can taste. His mob rev up the chainsaws

while he lectures the cops, checks how their loyalties lie.
A sniff of defection incites him to pick up a plank and

batter her, hammer her head and her belly to plasma.
Her plummeting brain remembers that crux, *Laredo.*

Little Queen

'Will I be buried in my victim's skin?'
– Malika Oufkir

The freewoman gains a token majesty in a closet
barely twice her size. Self-sentenced for the regulation
5.5 hours, she daily interviews the dispossessed.

Varifocals re-inforce the protective glass panel
and the ex-prisoner sees a common ground.
How far from here to Tazmamart?

King Hassan called the jail a collective delusion,
and convinced very few. The chainless, Malika thinks,
delude themselves to more convenient cages.

Once companion to a princess, she has a royal manner,
waits all day for a seneschal, before approaching
the civil servant in her re-inforced cell.

When records and identity collapse, the lizard may
emerge, or the ant. Or, maybe, the fluent woman
who talked herself alive for 1001 nights.

Malika conjured a tale of Russia in a
South Morocco jail for 5.5 times that.

the cockroaches of bir jdid

'We'd follow the progress of a cockroach from one hole in the wall to another'

– Malika Oufkir

they upscuttle. they will overcome.
they freeze-frame her with their caca-trail.
with their cacaphon -icscratch they bare her.
horizontal hostess. white as a concubine's house.

they rename her: homeland; castle atlas;
nightly date. to tease, dump on, demote.
they relay longevitous, hunt headless.
her anus cruxifies her, bleeds her anorexic.

she picks droppings off bread. what's to eat?
eggshells phlegm-green and murken inside.
she's a pustule that won't be cracked. her lush hair
self-sheds and a shard of mirror screams death.

her body is not its own mistress.
though all pale-gummy and vanished molars,
it will fight the sardine tin's fatal slice.
the roaches are waiters, serving nothing but their time.

SMALLED

'He even denied me my reflection in the mirror'
– Natascha Kampusch

Maestro is everywhere, a non-reactive gas. Rides on O_2
through the narrow pipe, all the way from the house.

She has been smalled. Her fat is fallen from pure lack,
the horizon squared to a twenty-pace perimeter.

She's his. He hers, maybe, except it seems he chose.
He can slam her hand against a sink and leave a scar.

He arrives where she doesn't want, his body a hound,
but he's predictable (nothing as tedious as a marauder).

He kneels on her breasts, slams her head on the floor, so
she launches it as satellite, to spy. She, there, hurts.

He is the one, oversees her pee, and the other. At least
she never doubts she's wanted, always plays a role.

Obey, Obey, he monotones. What can she, Punch-bag, do?
But small can morph. In time's sight, a larger lurks.

The wall must be felled, she prays to the arbitrary dark.
She'll reduce him, and then for the licking of his bones.

CUT

'Love hurts three times – when they cut you, when you are married and when you give birth'
– Waris Dirie

prune is the ugly of plum, as scarified jowl to the smooth,
deadened eyes to the wide unbelieving limbprisoned.

here she comes in the rubric heat with her dishnblade
her gap-fingered hand her thorns and her shady slouch.

plain is the pretty of prinks to the fisherman's eye.
cleaner the corpse of flutter and wing in the swathe.

here comes the pinched virgin rung by a tinnital bell
in her muffled hood in the teardrop shrine unboned.

grace is the cut dog in the cave of the crimson scream,
in the writhe of her tongue and the teeth gone slop.

here they come dolloping pain in the blindfold bowl
of the beggared daughter dot in the humdrunk drum.

rich the sculpted child of the master carve, with her place
in the house. poor is the hut of a knifeless god.

there she goes speared by a hunter's thorn in a painted
face, in a string of bloods and a fundal chain.

net

'Your face is ridiculous: O. . . . . leeeeee ugly :) <3 / thanks,
sure i know !:L'
– Ciara Pugsley, *ask.fm*

whn th little lite shinin frm abve doesnt
n younguns mad fr luv r spected 2 b home
thumbs go drum on magic pads n open windows
so they travel in thr dreambots huntin souls
they go weft upon th crystal warp unshuttled
hookin up witout a plan 2 build a planet
trances risin tru th base n snare of ask n tell
wot u c is wot u feel n wot u feels rite
tho snot a total giggle when th trolls r out
– no1 knows th cause like with any freakin demic –
bitch please u aint jesus wots wit all the posin
howd u like my cock up ur ass u cross-eyed ho

som1 feelin tiny in the sprawlin fabric
hauls back in2 her drum for a re-birth much 2 brite
bodys blinded so her double takes it weepin
2 th woods
to be an hero
wit a reel
hank
o rope

SEIZED

'Did he rape my head, too?'
– Laurie Halse Anderson

flesh is not for slicing except dead meat

so don't with your long hard-as-iron

– you can't – push until the lock breaks

because me is living down there

and me is insect squashable   i know that now

what will i do or what kind of human will i

if you slice off my breast and plough so deep

the soft soil my very root never heals over

i've read of a girl hung by her nipples

how would you bear that   stop   you don't

i'm a bad story and a dirty dream   slush

a tooth out   blood where my flesh slivered

pit of tearing claws where i was tight tunnel

doesn't matter why   you're the whole matrix

a razor topped fence   pain has remade me

raw as disembowelled   as a mouthless flapping fish

Daughter-Giant feels a swell of movement. Her mother's tides. They sometimes abate to total stillness, but can rise to a great brawl of eddies and undertows. She prefers the storm to the calm, because she is accompanied then. Oh, she is large and accompanies herself, with all her communicating parts, but it is not enough. When her mother is silent, this big daughter mourns as she moves, listening all the while for sounds of awakening.

'Mother?'

'Yes, Daughter?' Voice clear as silver.

What was the question?

'Where is this happening? I cannot place it in myself or in you. I know the countries in her dreams, but not where she dreams them'.

'It's happening in you, Daughter, if you see it'.

'But the signals, these scenes, might originate elsewhere …' She has no idea how.

'You forget that it's your eye in the box. You must judge for yourself'.

Now it is Daughter's turn to become turbulent. She suffers a great convulsion and for a moment the screen blurs. Places occur in her like random thoughts, without roads or signposts to connect them, so she has no idea where anything is, and cannot begin to build a map.

'Watch with me, Mother'.

Mother smiles and turns her tides to other things.

WITNESS

'Either the family does not pursue such cases or police don't properly investigate'
– Zia Awan

The woman's room is a grain of absence, like desert.
Her face is unsteady; it should look somewhere, but the
window has little to reveal and movement stings.

He will be home soon, with his seneschal of anger,
and she will not resist. There's a faint in her stomach
like the unstanchable draining of an etheric ichor.

She is full only of body. Her distant family is finished
with her. She has been honourably dispatched.
Whatever was promised in the magic shapes of cumuli

has been eclipsed by a browsing of lattice-dulled light.
The kingdom of pain loves her intimations, clasps
them to its chest of thorns, red the colour of meat.

She scorns lipstick, bears witness by limp and pall.
A girl screams in the town square. She must die by
degrees, like her passion. *Large stones kill too quickly,*
but pebbles are not stones. The head is left for last.

Woman and Frog

'When sperm has gone cold, how horrible'
– Pauline Bewick

Frog crept up her passage and into her spawn-house.
At first suavely inscrutable, he grew simply selfish
in the dark, squatted, all that way in.
Once home, he threw off his skin and hopped about.

Decorating. Slime green and cold semen cream.
A conceptual coup. Mikes in her face, no comment,
too deeply infiltrated to summon resistance.
His sticky warted suit her thick nuptial cloak.

He clamped his feet to her wall. Her skin plumbed
the grooves in his sole, became his stamping ground.
She played alive and he thought to clasp her shut,
behind an oozing, drawbridged, elegant abut.

She wept enough to think herself amphibian.
They drank to each other – secreting, shooting up.
She slept, breathing loud, dreamed she had birthed
on the grass, beside the lake, a new him.

HIDE

'It was very easy to die in Auschwitz. Surviving was a full time job'
– Eva Kor

As the needle pierced her cornea, Iris disappeared.
Down the many tributaries of her body, speedboating.

Peering into all those rooms again that made her child.
China dolls not made of boneash but themselves.

She elved from hoisted arms to cavort in silver trees,
then became an Amazon's bow; though hard, it bends.

Feverish unhuman in the brief night, she became
a firefly's cold burning in the woods near Nuremberg.

They wrote *Gestapo* on her until she was pergament
and history. She made of it her exegetic bonescript.

Held her cheeks like Dietrich in the photograph.
Naked or not, there are coverts and the veil of a face.

Look, says Parvit, *don'tlook. I am just one, norace,*
nobody. Noseless, geneless, wealthless, skilless, mute.

In my dark niche I am noglow and below your sweep,
will preserve all that I am unabscessed, if unformed.

Giant's Daughter's daughter-eye shifts in its box. Daughter ruffles round it, restless, but held by Giant's superior will.

'She dreams of lives, but she lives none', she complains. She examines the scene for signs that something might happen. She presses against her encompassing mother, wanting her to stay, close. 'She's too still. There's no story if nothing is done'.

Giant takes a long breath.

'Something will be done. Something is always done'.

Parvit Awake

She Dwells

Home's not where heart beats, unless body is home,
then Parvit owns something, but not the ceiling
she paints with intimate brushes in her body's ooze.
She curls beneath it, having no will to stake a claim.

Here's a tour of where she dwells, a curious inventory:
vertical rift in the wall's layers, letting a lizard of light;
a room cleft off this, cul-de-sacced by stone and fall;
designs she has etched above – in rare focused bouts –
of flowers, shells, snakes, labyrinths round and square;
a bowl-shaped groove beneath, unwittingly made.

Shapeless, she doesn't walk, but shifts and twists,
pushing the jetsam of her carvings onto the floor
next the gap. Shards, dust, brushings from her skin,
collect and tip over. In brief recognitions, she's aware
that it's the plight of a prisoner to live with her waste.

On the street side, a blank slab masks her living crypt.

Off-Grid

Often, in her abeyance, Parvit feels the grid of Agelast
illume and heat, designing a chessboard on her slump.
White's consort in danger from Black's officer; she retreats.
Black's officer snaps up miner; hierarch on the diagonal.
Check.

A face per square, others behind like stacked cards,
picked in sequence by an unseen croupier's hand;
replaced by more, a water-table of them, seeping up.
She cowers. Pretty Parvit. Singular Parvit. I.D. is theft.
Cut.

Agelastians behave according to their modes. Free
is not a concept, so neither is its opposite. Databases,
fed by sensors on the streets, diagnose the public state.
A skipping tread? Levity. A raised voice? Stridentosis.
index.dat.

Lacking blanket, Parvit snuggles in herself, insulates.

POD

Agelast is never mute. Parvit, perched ten micro-urges
from Ground and sandwiched in the slate, is head-and-
footered by a diligence of noise – hammers, drills,
mechanical cutters, blasts to excavate the stone.

For sixteen urgons down, devices hack and slice and
pull ore from dense graves. Hauled through adits
up to the urban edges, the gleanings are paraded
through the city, like an ant army's march home.

Mine-focus subverts vision. Ground on top, Sky passive
and vacant. Products ensue. Parvit tracks the industry
to smelting plants and factories between the streets,
then up the articulate towers, to its commercial cry.

She's a small dissenting nerve in this saccadic brain,
a feigning crush among the crannies of its folds.
Kinless in the adamant scrapings of an echoing pod,
princess in the sour pulp of an inedible, imploding pea.

Parvit Recalls Her Outer Self

Nothing was ever always like this.
Nor was Parvit always in slump.
She's a loser of something
she hounds her brainself to recall.
Sharp fragments inhabit her, pinching
at random, itching to connect. They're

white and brittle, lighter than fingernails,
harder than dry leaves. She dreams a container
with slop inside until there's bubbling heat,
then coagulum quick. Thickened Parvit.
Parvit ready-to-eat. Parvit exposed.
Her throatself gags as she swallows.

Crack and dissolution. The whole shell ingested
like stitches, bedding its bitter shards higgledy.
Spiked Parvit, nothing showing but all abristle.
Plainly, this is not how it was meant.

Giant's Daughter sends part of her mind rippling over other locations, contemplating herself. She's a vast hive of worlds, each of them a discrete unit at work within her massive, conglomerate breathing. Is this what Parvit is doing – travelling within herself? But she is so small and encaged, only aware of what she is not. Daughter-Giant is full to the brim with movement and memory, whereas Parvit contains only lack. She has neither function nor possibility, an outsider in every degree – outside her body, outside the city in which she is so intimately embedded.

She is hardly of importance, Daughter thinks, *having such a negative existence. I may find myself slowing in all parts if this eye remains attached.*

'Small things might seem unimportant', her mother says, 'but if ignored they often become larger'.

'Like cancer', Daughter mutters, wondering if Mother can read her thoughts.

'Like change', Giant says.

THE GELBEN TRANSPORTATIONS

GELB

Watching from above the permanent cloud called Sky,
you might yourself be gelb, a feel of yellow seeping in
from somewhere behind.

The curdle thins. You see its pores. Your skin responds
in probing fingers. The whole mass shudders,
bares its humps and hollows.

Though smaller than the cloud, you can rule it by its
own will. Your heat grows with each infiltrating touch,
until you riddle it with scorching spears.

No notion but a burning mission. You concentrate,
gather force. You think yourself a bomber, but as you
rev, you know with certainty you are the bomb.

Compulsive. No backing out. Full gelb must blow.
Unkeepable secret, brakeless train of pregnancy,
poised predator, finally it's lizard-quick. Lets off 256
gaseous gimlets with the vicious unconcern of a god.

parvit in gelb

rising in gelben urgency.
hail of pinpricks the skin is.
what skin? vanished in fluid fire.
little parvit possessed by something bright.

this is your tonight cloak,
joined by dots, a red voile damascene.
black star of pain round each bore.
this is too electric to be agelast.

no way to lie on the burning ledge.
she rolls and knows that she is entity,
has relation and remove, a harder
cohesion, heated to purpose.

aware for a minute and palpitating.
he will see her now with his tyrant beam.
but no, his every watcher is bound to barracks,
disabled, as fledgling parvit is taken to the air.

Parvit Halts at the Towers

There's nowhere to perch that doesn't pierce.
Parvit stalls in the air beside a long steel spire,
then drops abreast the tower's polished sides.
Slate smoothness and albuminous could be a match,
but she shivers to her ubiquitous core,
the long note of history forking through her.
These japanned slices of the past, these
tenebrous resolutions, both attract and repel.
Existence voids of all except itself, her last white
melts to mush and helplessly she sticks to the slate.

No no, Parvit flows. She is flexible, amorphous,
all roll, no rock, her voice a clear, unalloyed note.
She stretches to gelb with her diffident will and finds
propulsion. Muscle-tight, capillary action high, she
rockets up a yellow straw luciferous, through the
cloudcap, in an anti-Agelastian operation.

Beyond the White Sky
(The World According to Parvit, Cloud)

This planet I survey was always the same, just differently
organised, producing and devouring itself,
endlessly. There's no such nature here as square.

Me on no map, just floating over billions of lights
and insistent seas. The waves keep you sharp, friends,
remind you not to cave in and bubbleise, be not Parvit.

But be-yearn to me with your pulses, feel for free.
Like she in the cellar behind the concrete door, beyond
the anteroom, without scissors or glue, tearfully

tearing crayoned hearts and sticking them with *Nivea*.
To mark. The day. Of her mother's birth. Under the
unleavened mattress they become her atomic clock.

She, chained in the Columbian jungle, whose father
told her to use each political second, says the Rosary
every noon because far away Mama does too. I, Parvit,
am true pole mother, over and above these gestures,
dispersed in the extreme. Therefore in the sea a buoy.

she sings within walls

she has a blue voice and sings gentian violet
she has a voice crimson and sunflower yellow
she strikes tones of orange wood parquet
and laces them with eighteen carat gold

keys curve in on themselves and become eggs
burst upward purple spirals and climb
utterly from her stemble limbs her layers
her sharps twingling her sub-softs brustling

the gray ceiling marbles with her oh feel
white strings draw leafgreen catkin nutbrown
rose and peony until landscaped she is
a vast field of blossom forgetting the hard

earth that is never sure of water that long-
forming substance that stops her being nothing
she sings within walls and becomes their out
their forgetter disclaims their every hold

Another Dimension

'I stared out the window and fantasized myself in different places, where I was doing something great'
– Tamara de Lempicka

'Ponder the impeccable square, paradigm
for almost all foundations. Crucial'.
Teacher tweaks his long robe,
slate-gray, predictably.

Tamara draws a square and within it
a labyrinth she thinks of as relief.
It threads upward from the plane,
a seven-coiled snake.

Chin upon her palm, her face
verts to the window and sky's
faux simplicity setting off
a glib girl in effervescent blue.

Launched from a four-square pad,
she reckons, a muscular form might reach
a solid loft on a shaking tree,
an iridescent resolution.

Dancing Girl, Kenmare

'... these paintings represent my instinctive way through this life'
– Pauline Bewick

little girl is not a tree
is twigs unbundled

is stray bones and limbs
a flailing rubber cross

under her sway nothing is weird
or wondered at no word opened

speckle in the silence of the main frame
if her stir is stored who knows

she is pliant in the purrpurr
shall she bind to herself anything

what's pressing in is tight but easy
she's a pore in it no a thread

come in for dinner says mother
sit on my lap says father

his hands gather her
his hands are cords

DEVIL'S WINE

'I hate to think about the men, now. They came from all walks of life'
– Lyn Madden

Bubbles unwrapped she is/ doesn't know herself//
All that deep delving and now she's popped//
The trapdoor's gone awol// she's unshelved/ un-
categorically out of the barrel/ cat in everyone's eye//

No avoidance/ laughs are nucleated/ she too//
It's a blast/ LED flûtes kitschly raised up to cheers//
Still golden when she rollercoasters down/ ambience
in a body/ doubly avatared/ gone to organ//

Lyn can't get enough of it/ perfect for a woman/
yeast out with the lees/ all tasteless froth blown off//
The yellow river he sprayed on her face is absolved
by this salving stream *in nomine nēmō / amen//*

Pills popped/ she's down countless/ Parvit dispersed
in her body even better/ Parvit's her new mother/
best friend/ on this holiday without a plane//
Now Lyn's the one hard-riding/ until fluidly erased//

mammy longlegs

'I named her Bianca and I would talk to her'
– Jaycee Dugard

you leave the ledge of terror by hiding underneath.
parvit spreads legs to the cracked wood, bestilled.
this body is a new yukon, its far tips a golden dream.
who knows what's beyond the high knees, or below?
she can feel her extremities like wet lips pressed
against a small input, birthing an instinctual map.
she sees the girl at the edge of her compound eye.
she has felt her delicate approach, her reverence.

the child has learned her topography by how it hurts.
he has blasted a long passage he mines without pause.
she wishes she had no treasure to pull cruel pilgrims,
like this cleverly private insect she names bianca.
the elegant tail, lucid wings, widely-spread legs,
are flourishes she might have made in a different skin.
a crane fly lives to mate, but parvit redesigns, becomes
the trapped girl's pet, sterile mother in the silent shed.

So she has moved, but not by her own will. Does Daughter-Giant move by her own will? She certainly wills herself to focus and re-focus, but the larger shiftings, the breathing and the weather, what wills them? She lives within her mother, who seeps into her betimes, so is it Giant that moves her?

She doesn't like excessive contemplation. It creates clumps. At least she has begun to see a story in this vision of Parvit, now that contact has been made with a world she knows.

'What is she composed of?'

'Something volatile, I suppose', says Giant, 'like mercury, but more solid and less poisonous'.

'Hmmm, messenger of the slate-god'.

'Maybe so, but she thinks she's the message'.

Proof of Life

'You feel your fear, but you accept it and you put it aside'
– Ingrid Betancourt

It's all for the saving of the seconds, so time
will not turn you to psychic pulp in the captive grind.
You decide coldly, but when the evening comes
and dogs in the twilight briefly look like wolves,
knees weaken and the close-by thicket swims in sweat.

Your preparation will keep you locked to steps,
one by one, and to each bending under a new branch.
You live your rehearsals like a god tentative in her
creation. Blueprint becomes flesh and compulsion,
the plan its own necessity, gelled to breath.

You transmute the metal of the stars, reflections cast
underfoot by a new moon; your lover's face becomes
the muscle that casts itself into the dive and swim.
Could you act without belief in a pure light, dust-free,
wired to a golden precedent? But action prods belief,
dares it prove what bead and book declare a legacy.

A Wearable Shade

'It was the lipstick and the pen that could have changed [the prisoners'] lives'
– Ingrid Betancourt

The missile teases open your hapless lips,
but instead of another bite that will land
you in more shitty prison, you realise, *foxy lady,*
you are being fêted with *succulent plum,*
so you can lay back and not fight this.
Think of your desirably undesired breasts,
disembodied *jelly-dongs, soft throbbers,*
yogurt slingers and the *one-eyed snakes* you,
Cleopatra, might de-fang, de-skin and wear
round your privately beautiful body. Purse
yourself like a savings account, invest your
payload in a frictional growth of riskless
unshares. Slip softly into the sweet picture,
lower your shoulders, watch colour resume
in your blistered face. Sores and scratches,
deep eye-beds, by these simple strokes outshone.

THREE GOOD REASONS TO BE A VIVIENNE WESTWOOD TARTAN DRESS

'It's quite incredible to think that we might be able to save the world through fashion'
– Vivienne Westwood

When global warming worsifies,
Earth will shrink incredibly to
Size 4 or so, a billion souls
Tightly squeezed on a patch of ground
West of the water, the measure
Of a Hermès dip-dye silk scarf.
Off the shoulder will be good, but
Diamante with long train, no.

Vivacity takes the biscuit
In all famines. Red crayon lines
Vie with wrinkles and brighten eyes.
In the Nairobi slums she mixed
Effluence with style to make bags
Nifty enough to fill with nothing.
Never wear knickers with a skirt.
Ewer twill says so much about ewe.

Virgin by Desire

'The vagina connects the uterus to the outside world'
– WebMD

Down there is much too vulvar for a parvitoid.
No, she's never looked, leaves it to be manhandled
and says, oh that's good, and, yes please, more –
then turns away and thinks of chocolate mousse.

She's fifty-three and at a *Wild Woman* day
feels tamer than a pet budgie, yellow as sour curds.
She puts a mirror on the floor, shrinks to a
sideways eye, and stands over it on uncertain feet.

What's fertile in black with the softest cliff edge?
A folded world in a taut rubber rim. She fingers.
More ground than she bargained for, less hold.
All that flapping woman and the real one so far in.

She draws back the outer skin and sees a shrine
isosceles: distinct virgin with hood, hands in a V.
Her belly quakes; of course it's true – she's pink
and innocent, inviolate, the fact where myth began.

post

'A man loves most everything about his wife when their sex life is good'
– David Bentley

iit's loverly lying headback on the pillow
after pee has hooked up with ooo 'n lollipopped.
such hardnfast sucking makes 'm reelly laugh.
'e goes neon yellow, fuschia 'n apple red,
'd vanish now blissly if she candleised, 'is hole self
'smelted down to bonerless ashenmath.

all the massive globe's crystal in 'is fulled-up head.
'e knows it all, rapped 'n ready for any other bee-ness.
Whatelse – no prob – needs straightening out orup,
or tucked away or brung to the table for deepprobe?
'e rules the roost, chest a larger measure than afore.
'ees a fed eagle's eye, full nest 'n lakewide wingspan.

'e papats the biceps on 'er right arm 'n squeezes,
meaning thank-you-unsayable-much plus good-on-ya.
'e wants to buy 'er somethingspice.
she's the happle pip of 'is iis.

Daughter-Giant squeezes herself in the pleasure-places and curves the hammocks of her mouths. Parvit delivers illusions, but all action is illusion once you finish it and move elsewhere. Flitting from present to present, ecstatic, Daughter circuits the marshy lakes of memory and the busy factories of truth.

BREATHARIAN

'The omnipresent Light ... keeps alive a person
who does not consume food'
– Joachim M. Werdin

Born to the concept of a round world, we are soon
rendered unwhole.
The fact is, bare breath swells and sends us through the
rib cage into
An immense nutritious ma'am, toll-free solar sustenance.
Essence of IAM pervades the cosmic particles
And cooks micro-love-food. What else is mother's milk?
I diminish to enlarge myself in her.
Gaia. Prana. Eating is metaphor.
I brook no medium. Straight to source.
Quantum field intelligence plus
Interdimensional light-
Beings turn our dis-ease
To world unity.
The more you starve
The less death.
Para
Dox

The Key to Paradise

'... the body of Wafa became shrapnel that eliminated despair and aroused hope'
– Adel Sadew

You will be saved from the place of no landmark,
will be no scapegoat under the frozen hot eye,
blister-backed, hairy, crunching backward to beast.

You will regain the ultimate kingdom of your source,
your beauty will be unsurpassed, and you will sit
on the right knee of a virtuous king, made subject
by your love. There will be bright-plumed birds and
four undying springs of milk, honey, oil and wine.

Your lover will adore you under the great tree; there
will be no touch without an ecstatic end that leaves
you warm and wed to the grass you collapse on.
There will be no argument, never pain. Balm will drip
from every leaf in this catchment of considerate sun.

And they will call you wise, not inessential. So gird
yourself with red rockets; blow your littler 'I' to the
garden of infinite fecundity. Do it. In one starry bang.

Gone

'I never paint dreams or nightmares. I paint my own reality'
– Frida Kahlo

Parvit is a glomerate of hope, buzzing through avatars.
Her thoughts are atomic spurts; not word not picture.
Her substance, what there is, feels its own way,
breathing in each new vessel the gelben breath.
No ruptures. A chain dance, sparking from one to one.

No nature too strange, no beginning beyond attempt.
One body is the lot, the principle of body, and none.
This world beyond the wall is infinite, she knows,
but, faceless, she only gains it by repeated lease,
her freedom bound to the claims of its opposite.

She parties on to dissolution and in sheer exuberance
believes her avatar can fly. Dive! she commands, and
the air absorbs them   it is allembrace   holds them
in its whistling limpid lung   is master like an easy do.

Parvit stops singing and the body suffers her mistake,
explodes on the pavement, bombing them apart.

return

all's bright, dazzling as a flame before demise.
parvit bursts apart, suspended in liminal terror.
once glutinous, now she's a swarm of gases,
swept from the death scene like a child.

with all her letting go in gelben communing,
all her snaky smooth of skin and tone, she
should marry this outgang with a gold ring,
you'd think, ride it with wild will, a harpy.

but this is transport with a duller gilt.
she's ransacked by it, she's avalanched.
gas she might be, but her pain is solid,
a new avatar, insensible and cinched.

when the hunter tires there's always home,
or what was the cot. if body balks, hope insists.
she makes no decision, being parvit, gets droned
through turbulent cloud, re-figured, back to agelast.

'Can she not choose?' Daughter-Giant cries. She has begun to empathise with amorphous, luminescent Parvit. 'Why was she pulled back? Capillary action shouldn't suck down. How can weather pursue someone beyond its region like a homing device?'

She becomes aware of the distance between her wordself and the cube and marvels at the way she feels what Daughter-eye shows her. She and Mother are large, but any part can contact another by the simple act of attention. This dispersed unity is the abiding mystery of their awareness.

Daughter feels ache in a cerebral region. Parvit would be giant if she could let her knowledge be her living; but she dwells only in the gaps between experiences, and that is no dwelling at all.

Mother is silent. Probably sleeping again. Daughter listens closely, but an anxious drumming pervades her, muddling the rhythm of Giant's breath.

The Risen Parvit

Home

Parvit's back in the mausoleum
but she's not out cold. She's an emporium
and the traffic's much too close for humdrum
denial. She has eyes that won't close or stem
their fascination with surrounding items,
like the perfect imperfections in the limning
of the stone above her head. Maximum
exposure finds her on feet, sanctum
bedamned. Incarnate with the minimum
of effort, what happened up to then
forgotten. The light is cruelly undimmed,
the slab that fronted her bed plumped
on its side, gossiping streets looming
at her haven's edge. Standing in the cleft, him,
serious and broad, the two locked in recognition,
staring at their opposites. Home is

Paramour

He wears deep purple and she vitellus.
He makes a sound and offers her a cloak.
Her lips boil open and freeze.
She finds herself belly-based,
it all churning in dark chews.

Her ears go down, sound-sorting,
decohered by the tone-tome, come up empty.
Words are statues in a hasty procession,
cargoed by stiffstance. The pitch, maybe, a thing.
Name? she hears, and fumbles. *Par... Par...*

He levels his palm and finds hers,
draws her out of the blown passage
onto a thoroughfare flagged by stares
and the hooded, polished faces of the Stern.
'This is Par', he rasps, 'my destined *amour*'.

A boon, she thinks, that someone knows the score.

Parade

Parvit is a young queen in a foreign land. Grizman
displays her like booty. Unaccustomed, her eyes don't
venture up, and she first learns Agelast with senses
tuned to low light and quiet. They praise her shyness.

She has a strange colour. Cloud plus glair of egg,
some think; but the Deft, who are artists, shift legs
and say she'll change in time – pink, then yellow, then
crystal white. To protect her skin, they offer her a veil.

She's beautiful, if clumsy, as though her feet
were not made to walk but dangle languid in a float.
A whisper goes that she's a sort of sprite, a fitting mate
for Grizman, bureaucrat supreme, epitome of Agelast.

They stand in an open car and the crowd swells.
News of the sleeper in the wall, woken by gelb, fills
the grid of screens and radios. The populace is thrilled
by its new child, risen unfertilised by some secret will.

WHERE THEY SHALL LIVE

The home tower is in the division of Archonbase.
'Where government officials and city leaders
make their homes', he says, and leaning to her ear,
swankily, 'I'm next in line for Dominus'.

Parvit lifts her eyes, scans the walls. They are grandly
ornate, incognate with her scratchings at the ledge.
Fine carvings of toolish objects and people at work.
'Symbols of production', Grizman says. 'Wonderful'.

'Wonderful', she repeats, wondered by the word.
Grizman names hammers and drills, miners and
metalworkers. Deft engineers with their masterplans,
Null labourers, puffed up alike by the city's pomps.

Round the cornices a rank of solemn, chiselled faces.
'The progenitors'. Sagely, he adds, 'They sustain us'.
Their quartz eyes with no irises unnerve her.
She sees herself tunnelling their bones, alien, torchless.

'She was nearly giant and now she's bone-bound. Poor victim. She'll have a single focus like all small beings'.

'Appearances can be deceptive', says Giant, breaking her long silence. 'Remember, the eye can only relate what it sees. Other senses will tell other things'.

'Like what – that she is large?' Daughter *humphs*.

'It's relative'.

'She can be seen from the outside. Anything finite is small. Anything finite is only one'.

'She is not hollow', Giant says gently. 'And if we cut her open, we would not find all that fills her'.

Getting to Know

Grizman stretches on his blood-red couch, observing.
She sits, absorbed by a compliant man-sized cushion.

'So'. 'How long have you been hidden in the grooves?
Is there a brood of you? Your parents in some burrow?'

Parvit teases his meaning. 'I', she stutters, 'I occur.
No other'. A pretty lie, he thinks. He'll bide his time.

He smiles. 'You glow'. 'You gleam', she replies.
His chest swells. Their eyes advance and retreat.

He won't rush her. She's a gem unpolished, will need
skilful honing to perfect. He prinks his satin robe.

She shivers at his touch. Hand never held, he reckons.
He only wants her close, and she comes, but her frame

tightens as if to bear a shock. He thinks of a small rabbit
huddled in the bushes between towers in Alpha.

They watch a movie and she's impressed, though guards
her reactions, like a soft ball studded with pins.

Adjustments

She sleeps best on the floor in an earth-brown blanket,
pressed to the wall, a slate pencil beside her. He permits
her primitive murals, but every night invites her
to his bed, guides her hand along the four exquisite
posts, coaxes her to the pillow.

The penthouse flat is high fashion, but it's not gelb.
Par unearthed is *over-she* and, like a committee, draws
to conclusions by the winding thread of verbal syntax.
Before, having and losing were the one spinning coin,
action its own decision, circumstance the life.

Grizman instructs her in slaten ways. He's amazed
at how she learns, her essence open as scaffolding.
She construes her face in every new square window,
begins to kiss him, re-enacting gelben savvy –
the dance of modes, the secrets in survival's brief.

He's convinced by her; she, sometimes, by herself.

DIET

There's nothing to eat that wouldn't, Parvit thinks,
turn her slate-like and obdurate, corporate gray.
He brings her a crimp-edged, lace-lined tray,
yellow flower in a wing-shaped vase to tempt her.

To green and crimson pills; dried pink meats;
a svelte cup of nutrient-thick, tasteless soup.
To him and his, the fare spells excellence and style,
but she dilutes to the marsh of her marrow and gags.

Powerless Parvit doesn't plan what might be cooked,
but strokes hunger till her palms are begging bowls.
Was there a time before the mouth became a worker,
when a dark, reliable host supplied without demand?

She conjures a loving giant, the cornucopian cord,
awakens her many pores to suck, autonomous each
in its non-aligned state. She grows large about them
and, risen again, accepts a crimson pill and ruminates.

Parvit Complies

Parvit shapeshifts to a smile. She can even do
the teeth – perfectly even and diplomatically blunt.
Because he's standing over her with his chest bare,
his hankering bulk blocking all other views.

His square hands believe in her. Skin whiter than Sky,
smoother than the Krone's glossy walls. She is dove,
snake, orebody. Her thoughts are cryptic as a future,
but he's a sort of tunneller, driven to explore.

She spreads herself. Her lips draw back and let him
everywhere. *Sweet love,* he gasps, *my promised vein.*
She takes his rhythm and moves to his motion,
a slow rain and a fast sea, that sends her nowhere.

There is nowhere to go. Rented, she inhabits him,
his cleaving and his adamant resolve. Particulates
in the insular power, lets his passion be her wall.
He draws back, duped and satisfied.

VISTA

At the panoramic window, his executive poise,
enhanced by a tailor-made, metal-gray suit.
He is still, hair sleek as rulers, hands clasped
at the small of his back, tower-tough legs at ease.

Below are the confident lives he makes possible.
Sacrifice augments him like a bud's hidden vault.
Self must succumb to species. He does what's right.
His gaze is benign as the god's, his knowledge arcane.

Measurements and predictions are his burden, only
known to the Three. *Cloak 'n dagger,* Par quips, who only
invests in herself. The city is his blood and body,
his artpiece, his brainchild, collaborative and singular.

With the pedagogue and high priest, he trades
in the hard currency of futures, complex matters.
He pays with stiffness and thinned sleep, plus her pink
rebellions. But then, she polishes nails and sings.

IDIOPHONE

He takes her to a soundfest at the Resonant Hall.
She puts her palm to the wall's overlapping scales
and pictures the flaps prised open, elements invading.
Inside, she's a crystal in the deep-blue crowd,
lambent satin in a matrix of tulle and dark velvet,
receiving scenes like these through string and wind:

Ants, red cocks of their walk, swarm triumphant on
a nulled populus. Sky creatures drop white bombs
on small globes, glibly winging forth. Propeller-
faced flowers turn long dregswigs to yellow to the
point and pause of slab-on-slab's unbearable truth.

The audience name the keys and map the structure,
tick off each done tune, impassive as chalkboards.
She starts when he nudges. From her purple pulp
a small screech. All heads turn. Disconcerted,
her self-links slip through the sound-blown gaps.

Complex

Parvit still doesn't know herself for a creature.
Movement is not the fact. Her hands and legs seem
agents in themselves. She no more feels her wall or centre
or angles from the axis than Ground's breath
knows itself, being always in the state of verb.

She's a thread captured by a claw of needles, nameless
in a gang of slaves, the work a whim in the mind
of a hidden master. But before assimilation, she'll push
herself in the path of a nail and hang. Come the dark,
she's off to a new boss, the past mumbling to its gag.

Release is collapse. She musters all her will in crawling
to the next waystation. Outwardly nothing changes –
so Grizman says – except hairstyle and couture.
Puzzling, how she sees transformation, and others
just a whimsical girl, consistently variant.

All too complex to dwell on. She drains another glass.

What kind of world is this, where experience and reality are not the same? The problem with a body, thinks Daughter-Giant, is that it's expected to reflect its inner happenings to those who are outside. But are the happenings truly within, or do they turn the self outward? All of Daughter's many events take place within her extensive self and she has no observer, except Mother (when she's awake); though she and Mother are more like tones than entities, and there is no real division.

Daughter listens, something that's becoming a habit. Tremors again, all over, and a mingling of colours in the smooth places. She should never have allowed Mother to seize her like this. She might as well have a bony body too.

Dream of an Odd Career

(After 'Woman, Water and Oak Tree', by Pauline Bewick)

He wears a reflective waistcoat and paints a white line
all the way up the gray street. *Run,* he says. He
doesn't turn. She stalls, until an audience crops up.
Eager mugs, allcolour flags. Flutters through her now.
Naked, may I? At the gun, she tightens and sprints.

Feet turn slate to flesh, wind is breath, muscles muster
pinpoints of light. She's a shot arrow, bow and quiver,
trajectory and sliced air. Breasts are lamps in a fast car,
hands are propellers. She inter-is; finishes in a flash.
Form is no use, too distant, so she splatters out of it.

Hopeless! his voice thuds. *Whatless?* asks Amorphous.
Lost the race. Left the track. Misdirected your career.
She lifts her face to a shower of leaves, grabs hold
of a swinging creeper that mimes a tree. Becomes
silence and liquid climb, no line to toe, all curl.

She pinks, blinds his stare with a long, raptured gaze.

Bad Behaviour

She is graceless. Lacks gratitude. And respect.
Rebellious quivering at the junctions of the ears.
Has brew instead of starter. She'll be langers by dessert.

He tries to catch her eye, but she's saccadic as a hen.
An oddity. Agrees with nothing, just smirks or stares.
He's pitied. She's lovely, but looks never won the lode.

What happened manners? No erect back and gentle toast
as she raises her pill-bowl and delicately bites the fare.
No. She sniffs the pabulum, shudders and gulps it.

The women stiffen and strike her off their list of whos.
Grizman almost chokes; belly and heart collide. He takes
a long swig of follow-fluid and wishes for an alter-ego.

What to do? He can't give her up without disgrace.
Or pain. Her skin is woven silk, her smell is jasmine.
Well, better to mine and die than never try the face.

She finishes first. Makes no excuse to leave the table.

A Meeting of the Inner Council

Parvit's quorum skirt barely covers pleasure-trove and
pattocks. She banks her meshclad femurs under the table
for the bureaumeet, but all note their attendance. Every
second blink draws them to some part of her – the
specimen. Even the hierarch's holy eyes are made roam.

Ahems and coughs. They begin discoursing on the nature
of progress. Ground's core has delivered its gems. Might
Sky now be mined, instruments designed to navigate
its elements, in spite of gelb, or taming it? Anywhere else
the thought would be treason, but not in this godroom.

As they talk, they swivel eyes, scanning her response.
Dull, unbounceable words denerve her. She doodles.
The scientists itch to wire her up, the doctors to sedate,
the pedagogue to probe, the hierarch to instruct and fuse.
Her mystery is a needle, her presence a type of sweat.

If she weren't Grizman's pet, they'd have her for meat.

Grizman is Master of Mines, monitors the father lode,
trundles his significant mass down skinny shafts,
to record the gain, the waste, and what remains.
He walks humbly with the miners, Null included.

On inspection day he's well prepared. Mollimilk with
a vitamin-loaded breakfast cools his trepidations, lifts
the tension in his head. Once encased in the respirator
and protective suit, he fervently invokes the city-god

before stepping into the monorail transporter.
He sees the gaps in the strata long before the engineer
points them out. No mollimilk soothes fear of collapse,
but he chatters and recites Ground's benevolence.

At end-of-shift, medics adjust the levels of enhancol,
curbing the risk of discontent. Mining families
are the happiest. Engineers have expensive hobbies and
gorgeous, pampered wives; they're slow to procreate.

Extravagence

The curtains are from *Stylus* of Daedelwick. Top notch.
The cutlery too, delph and furnishings, the carpet.
Grizman stares as she unbubble-wraps a huge urn.

'Oh', she croons, 'how absolutely, how unbelievably.
Look at the fine structure and the ear-shaped handles.
I met the craftsman, you know. They took a picture'.

'They took a picture? For a newsfeed?' She nods
and strokes her craftefact. He becomes a stark dismay,
one allover spat-in eye. 'Are you nulled? Bad

enough to squander, but letting everyone see!
Government officials (you know well) mustn't behave
like Glib, or the moneybags of Cacaton'.

'I'm supporting craft. And I'm not an official'.
He feels stabbed. 'You're my wife'. 'Your paramour',
she corrects. 'Right. Even worse'. She grabs the
bubble wrap, curses every air-filled half world.

Unsettled

Hard as the skeleton is, Parvit would prefer a shell.
Armour is incomplete where the skin shows.

The house is entirely his. She has never settled in,
regardless of her pictures and her potterings.

How do you shift a stubborn history?
The broken egg sticks to the greaseless pan.

She is hankering for a true home and truest
are the tiny things – a speck of dust in light,

a snail on a path, a painted fingernail.
She likes herself in skimpy dresses.

Will she ever get squared? Look at Pyra next door,
quest-eyed and assured, managing a school.

Parvit lives wherever she feels, then forgets.
No position is precious. She gets snagged

on every prevalent assumption; none seems right.
Though in this, she might not be wrong.

'It's clear she's Ground-born. You saw the passage.
The scratchings are indelible. Experts agree the ledge
bears the marks of at least two generations'. Grizman
pauses for effect, but Cineron is blank as his portrait.

The pedagogue's words come in a slow march, eyes
on Grizman's flushed face. 'All creatures are Ground-
born, but she is hardly parentless, even if a subversive.
She is at least suspicious, too much unexplained'.

He lizard-blinks. 'You know the level of interest,
and the rumours?' Yes. 'They say she is Sky-spawn,
or that she is a new kind of nature. It's only one step
more to treason, if they construe something beyond'.

Grizman swallows and reminds him of the evidence.
Cineron gives his Dominus nod. 'She must submit
to study, and discretion. Misinform her of delicate
matters. No more public parades. Keep her in'.

Daughter-Giant flickers across herself in a series of quick, chasing lights. She loves all her parts and lives as much in pain as she does in pleasure. Maybe this is because her constitution is soft, with the nature of a viscous fluid. But some of her worlds are impervious and private, and may have harsh attitudes that she cannot detect. Maybe Agelast is hidden away in one of her bellies, disguised as an enzyme. The thought disturbs her. She vows to go exploring more deeply in herself when the show is over.

UNCOMMERCIAL

Parvit needs nottin, she thinks, denies her body ev'n,
so nowan can say, *Her legs are worth a million!*
Nowan can price her an'thin, so she's priceless.
Isn't everywan? When are the tags slapped on?

She listens to the chingching,
the bargainin, the boasts of bein somethin
or somewan, as if they could be nottin too.
Like a cityful of busy knives, hackin.

What you do is what you are, that's the jingle.
No talk without an answer to the question, a handle.
Parvit does breathin and core-travel and resistin.
She's a waster reelly, they're decidin over drinks,

clinkin glasses down the pub, their reward for workin.
They might just allow that she's a poor thing (nottin),
can't get herself together. (But in truth, she's stickin
together all too much, like an ore-body before blastin).

Parvit's Vision of a Sea

not liquid but rolling nonetheless
every move of finger is a current
hand a larger current and the body a squall
the whole not equal to a poly-partnered wave of
fingers hands and twin joined to twin ad infinitum

breakers she can't see pullnpush her
she performs for them like puppets
does domino-dives to slowmo far flips
quakes at speed-of-wave new ruptions
why she wakes at night pulsating and hothot

she can't look at the large picture
without tons weighing her down
no-one really knows the bottom of the sea
or the mind of an unembraceable drop
she could be liquid the way she so easily cries

she could be rock the way his talk leaves her unmoved.

Salivation

Cuisine is not an art but a science of synthesis.
Meals are pill ingestions, meat chiefly for the miners –
salted shards of small pigs kept on ground floors.

What's not conceived can't be desired. But in select
apartments of Archonbase, secret salivation binds
the men of power in a heady conspiracy of taste.

One food pampers the palate and calls up visions
in these dry citizens. Pink as an inner lip, it loosens
on the tongue and spurts its former life into every cell.

This is not for the mediocre. Even the grandees
have prescribed a liturgy to armour the psyche,
as they open to communion with flesh of their like.

'These whom we eat are our beloved', Kayman,
the hierarch, chants. 'They sanctify our blood. By them
we transcend our death and re-enact creation.

Eat and be eaten. Do this in recollection of ourselves'.

Disposal

It's a kind of love. The city lifts its refuse to the wall
and shoots it into the acquiescent, unthinkable beyond.
Cranes deliver to the towertops, where other cranes cast.
It's a ritual, dipping at the high heaps, backing, turning;
slow tips, rhythmic clanks, the reverent hum of engines.

Households waste little. Penalties are too severe. Mostly
it's dry tailings from the mines – rocks, overburden, what
was backfill, before the city's underbelly grew clogged.
Then there's the effluent, consequence of foreplay (build-
up, close labour, presentation of gems). In the nethers,

fluid is pneumatically pumped through the tight
apertures of pipes, to the same inexhaustible oblivion.
Agelast is eternal present, self-raptured, fixed at its
original 256 points, webbed in its own stirrings,
recycling them, sloughing off all stray concerns.

There is no wasteland.

Parvit at Large

Out

It was a drunken dream and she wakes in its mouth.
It was all mouth, hers, dropping to her knees, letting
every edible thing in. She needs more than she has.

Lying under the masseuse, her throat struggles
to dam a foul upsurge. That's all there is these days,
keeping the nausea down, containing herself.

Other lives whirr happily, like oiled machines.
She knows this mostly from video and TV. No
hesitant speeches, no wary arrivals and guilty exits.

These days she must shop in disguise, wearing a wig
and the coarse work-suit of the unprivileged. She peers
at the marketplace like a pig at a butcher's knife.

She's dressed. Her so-called maid, discreetly armed
with stun gun and mace, is busy at the door. A Null
wants admission to the penthouse. *Let him in,* she thinks,
and slips into the private lift, swift as instinct.

Alarm

She's jolted by a pulsing whine as the main doors part.
Barely through when the steel shutter crashes down
and settles in a final heave. There will be no return.

She scuttles down the street, pulse pounding, darts
into the next tower, among officials home for tea. But
she could be trapped, so scrambles out and snakes

through waves of gray faces. All those measured steps
forenenst her. She fixes on the Krone, wills it a haven.
Cars with sirens angle the rush hour jam. Her legs

weaken, but she hurries on, resisting a run, holding her
hood closed at the neck, looking at the pavement.
What exactly does she fear? He has never been cruel.

They'll bring an airborne, she reckons, and identify her
odd light. She feels the street behind resume its calm.
The police cars return. 'Faulty alarm', they call through
megaphones. 'Have a good evening. Safe home'.

Rounding the Krone

The street is long, like the view from path to spire.
It's level, but seems inclined. She wishes more speed.

The city grows leisurely in the seeping dark, lamps
and windows kindle to points; a face under a dim cap.

She the nose, pressing on. To the goal, and not goal.
The key, because she must go round the pyramid.

The Circus is mercifully thronged. She merges with the
pilgrims at the base of the steps, eases through.

A diviner in a tidal gown locks her in a lace of beads.
Her palm is scanned, then one wrist clasped in a cuff.

The crowd saves her. A wave displaces the woman
and Parvit's away, a needle through puckered cloth.

At last on the opposite side, she stops. They'll expect her
in Theta or Beta, but never in Alpha's anarchy.

She turns to lower-left, takes the second street, hardly
believes the dull metal sign that reads, *Severrund*.

Daughter-Giant nudges her mother. She has an ocean of questions and Mother has answered very few.
'Could a city this hard reside in a giant soft as I am?' she asks.
Giant gives a large, convulsive laugh, creating a wash in her daughter.
'What's funny?'
'You're only as soft as your next hard place, Daughter dear'.
'I think if this city lived in me, I'd feel it like a shard. It would hurt'.
'Ah, now you underestimate your softness'.
When did Mother get so cryptic?

Company

The plan is the same, its execution shabbier.
The towers of Alpha sector can't carry themselves.
She likes the lack of style, as she totters
past droop-eyed pedlars and women
with children strung at their necks.

She pushes the dangling cuff under her sleeve.
Soon she must find a hiding-place
and some renegade with a hacksaw.
A looping whistle makes her jerk around
and she measles with chimeric recall.

Red ooze, or the sense of it, spiders across the scene,
drapes its fingers on an ogling corner-gang.
Everything deforms. The towers shift and gossip.
She calls it illusion and greets the guys with a story.
They snigger and oblige; then take her to a
junk-strewn alley for a tab and a feed of beer.

Their Every Drop

This doesn't really happen does it? Not to women
minding their own busy   their selves   their walk   their
nessness. Really she's not here but back
in the penthouse with her feet up and the servant who's
actually a jailor is massaging her neck.
That's good yes. She takes wide breaths because pleasure
and pain are very close and you bear
them both by the depth of your chest-heaves.

Ahbutitishappeningbecausethisisascream not a sigh
forced from her every nook. It's a re-enactment now she
sees it of a dream she had when dreams were real. Where
did she lose her runlessness and become wide awake?
They don't see her as a pain-receiver just a
them-vessel so they pour in what they have and poor
Parvit is so spongy she lives their every drop
of casual ignorance, that most cruel thing.

Sympathy

Observing her with its eight efficient eyes. Motionless.
Placing her shape on the crepuscular map. Assessing.

Is she broken? Her nether parts are throbbing and hot.
Her legs are bow-bent. She could be a swiped spider.

This one is hale, abseiling from the shadow of a shelf.
She can't look up. Pain is the new word for movement.

The new word for escape is foolishness. To be chained
on a satin couch is freer than naked on a thoroughfare.

Where is he, her man of substance, her satin jailor?
He'll seek her in craft and couture, in dilettante bars.

He'd sweep her to his pillar-chest, she thinks.
She's his foil and foible, his inevitable, his nuance.

An onslaught of footsteps. She wishes on the spider,
forces herself up, heart a battle-drum requiring it.

A puffing woman, with bellows for a body, bends to her.
That kindly frown would plumb a well. She weeps.

Touch

The woman's eyes are tragedy. Her hands are aloe.
She applies the lotion like a mother, sending
prayers and imprecations through a chink of lips.

Agelast, who, allknowing, feels our every pain,
heal this wounded being, victim of illdeed.
Oh god, whose eye is ever closed, to whom intentions
are pre-known, recompense us, renew us, restore.

She's a toucher, seldom touched, a worshipper.
She's a resonating vessel, she's a channel. She
is large to Parvit, whom she childens in her sight.

Sacred Krone, our city's guardian, seek the sinner;
spear the sin and purge it, like our daily waste.
Away, you foulness, from the four divisions! Foulness burn!
Foulness go crying over the end-of-all wall!

She casts a salt circle, sprinkles rose-water,
strokes her new daughter's hair, turns her crystal.

It's red in Rosie's apartment (Rosie-red).
Such a cosy-up smell. Parvit is cuddled
(under-cuddled Parvit of the lone bed).
It's a world of dim and dreaming (swim right in).
Cheap damask drapings, cute figurines.
Must be nice to be a Null, easy standards,
clutter and camaraderie, cups of sweet tea,
reams of photographs (sentiment is history).
Lampshades have large-petalled flowers
that clash with ridiculous wallpaper stems.
Everything biggish, bright and buyable
at the local have-it-all store for a song.
Rosie has a hundred children plus three towers
and still counting. Parvit re-inclines herself
as a protector, pragmatic activist. These people
are under-rated, but, she pledges, not by her.

ADDICTION

Love without conditions is a pathless neighbourhood.
Rosie is often in bed. She holds court in it, wheezing,
watches mining dramas on the unaffordable TV.
She'll cry with all your troubles, rub your back, issue
interdicts in a shocked tone, then submerge them
in a lifedeep bowl of hard, irredeemable memories.

Everything clings to Rosie, in her puddle-self.
No-one leaves or changes her way. Total loyalty
works like metamorphic time – what is, solidifies.
Her dependants revisit pain and improbabilities,
mazes of dead ends, the swinging labrys of love,
the drug's broad, unending boulevard.

Parvit has never had a gang, so she overdoses
on drop-ins and close conversations. She carouses
in concealed venues, leans up against a wall with joint
or tab, the searing jab of a needle mostly demurred.

Rare

There's nothing to do but talk. Parvit's lonely past is a
rescued gem. They can't assess its value, but it gleams
amid the crush and they polish it as best they can.
Such a rare complexion. Is she of the slate at all?
They turn their heads sideways, shy of looking up.
Parvit lowers her chin, thinking to be modest.
She's prettier than them, uncommon, better spoken,
assumes a high place in this low order.

She unremembers how the rapers must have seen her.
Fallen walker, legs apart, she could have been anyone.
She upstages Rosie and plays oracle to fruit-eyed girls,
sandwiches liberation between laughs, while subtly
noting breasts and bulges, and the curious power
of a confident phrase to induce a pledged heart.
They think it's her heart makes her go with a Glib man.
It's his air of privilege, his promise, his silvery hands.

Does Parvit love her pain too? Daughter is not particularly sympathetic, though she has lived sympathy among her many points of involvement. Between these points she blankly breathes and tides, letting all her constituents behave according to their modes. There are destructions, she knows, battles and encagements, but overall she has no opinion on them. What happens is what must. She feels Parvit's deficiency, though, that she is not large enough to encompass her phenomena. She wishes her a fat snake with a pocket for everything that comes.

A New Protector

Welcome to Theta

It's where the glamorous go and she, he says, is stunning.
She'll outgleam the whole gang with that blaze-red hair,
those piercings and the tell-it-all dress beneath her cloak.

The Sateset atmosquare is a bubble-sea dropping colour.
Towers twist and gather light. It's nothing like Gamma.
Will she always be transported? she doesn't ask, and is.

In the club, glitter-clothed women do slow hand-stands,
use men as hinges and point their legs tower-high.
When all is revealed, it's like you see nothing.

Rubber male members with an inner life come leaping
at her from vendors, their fingers all reach and bling.
Whatever happens happens, that's the rule, with bells.

Parvit doesn't know she's being had. Doesn't think at all,
now she's taken a long drag from a tasselled pipe on a
blueandgoldglassandporcelain lookslikeamagic lamp.
All the new girls are having it.

MEANWHILE

Grizman watches the city. It breathes around him,
self-absorbed. He ruminates with it, attempting
by sympathetic magic to discover her location.

It is an hour to dawn. Wall and Sky coalesce
like faithful mates. It is in silence we commune best.
Later, elements will know each other only by striation.

Little Par. Lost within the great tangle and crush.
He has an image of her mystified eyes, gorgeous.
But they blink and transform, prismic with flirtation.

She's with a charmer, gold ring on his rivulent hand,
feeding her alien pills. She might be all too well found,
clinking with an accomplice to her plan's perfection.

The sector walls are too high to see beyond, or scale,
but within her freaky flesh she may have hidden pupal
wings, like a moth secretly maturing. In consternation

he showers, angling for a plan to recover his creation.

Strategy

'It's delicate', says Grizman, at another window
in another penthouse of Archonbase – *Adamant Office,*
administrative centre of the autopoietic regime.

'Like an insect's leg', the hierarch muses, voice low,
holy head bowed over the interactive map, his face
and Cineron's reflected in its rolling digital ream.

The hierarch is said to read minds, but Grizman knows
intelligence is the greater part of divine grace,
and the city's priests more scientific than they seem.

'Agents are posted in the sectors and divisions,
avoiding visibility for fear of unsettling the populace.
Short of death, her retrieval is only a matter of time'.

They plant indicators on the map, let him know
they suspect him, his mention of death regardless.
And he, who feels Agelast like his body, begins to
sweat, his structures threatened by a corrosive stream.

THIS TIME

… all she feels is an infused season of sea,
as if taken by rain's torrential philosophy,
this small room its cerebral source, this colliding
rhythm the pulse to its fierce flechette attack.

She's a prize, as always, her white skin saleable
(why he stole her) and, doped, she has no disgust.
Though, luckily, nous enough to take control,
play the artist, make the men her clients.

There is general satisfaction. He swells cloudy
in his suit like the flip side of Grizman;
as tall certainly and, it seems, the boss,
in this domain of painted eyes and ancient pus.

The men finish, but not rain. He sweeps her to his
muchtoolong white car and serves champagne in a
crystal flûte. They pullup in Dallhog outside a posh
tower with lavish chambers, a host of tinted views.

Daughter-Giant is bristling. Experience normally confined to pockets in her flexile substance is leaking into her smooth places and stippling them with sensation. Parvit is becoming sea in the wrong way. It's a reversal. The natural process is to consume, not disperse. But, Daughter reminds herself, Parvit is no giant. Perhaps she's not even a living entity, just an illusion stamped on the whirl by Mother.

To stanch the irritant ooze, Daughter tries to live all places at once and holds her breath. This causes folds and puckers, distorts the small worlds, turns them every which way. It gives her relief for as long as she holds, but when she lets go she is again beset by fingers of universal migration.

'Mother?' she calls.

There is no reply. The only sound is a new cacophony within herself, as her cells turn their minds to anarchy.

UNBROKEN

Whatness and whereness frisk the room. She blinks twice
and does a slow, considered survey. This is whoness,
waking in the Glib dawn a questioning eye.

Naked bodies in plastic and bronze, rounder parts
and apertures enhanced. Instruments of pleasurepain
hang like trophies among skewered lepidoptera.

She creeps to the bathroom, almost climbs the wall
of carpet and misreads the spouting golden snakes,
but her washed face shines like a new-lain, polished egg.

You have a boundary, says the nymph-ridden mirror.
She's already felt it in the satin sheet, her embedded
shell pressing outward, surprisingly coherent.

She can almost see her skin hardening to a sheath.
I am your crossing police, it tells her, *your tollgate.*
Living is better when the body is its own metropolis.
Parvit dresses silently as a cat and answers, *Yes.*

Groove

Doctor Love plays bendophone in a jasm band.
All the babes lie about the place – smokin'.
He wears a Sky-white suit, pressed 'n crispy,
and with a psychedelic shirt, he's an icon.
He totes half his fortune in his gemmy teeth,
on his fingers, 'n around his neck in chains.
He forgets to watch his body, doesn't have to,
when there's plenty supple sallys on his game.
He thinks they find his flabby belly sexy,
but it's habitude 'n homelessness in tune.
Little Parvit's not so minor as these leggies
with the sparkle on their eyelids 'n their boobs.
Now she's listenin' to her insides makin' plaster,
she's an artist with a universal view.
Men are all the same, she draws conclusion. They
can't tell fear 'n loathin' from the act of bein' true.

The Pellucid Zone

She will perform for him, *her dear,* at her own pace.
She has fine breakabilities. They must be practical.

She claims a separate bedroom and tells him the value
of a confidante, skilled in horizontal and vertical.

She decides she will not be a sally, but a sorceress,
her body a web of secret chambers with a helical

route to a selfish queen who will not show her face,
watching like a wary gambler in a dark follicle.

There are skills to hone, like the art of precise action.
She jolts from sleep, lamenting her loss of the possible.

Each day she finds a new facet for her world view.
She's a psychic snail, urging towards a kind of normal.

She studies common knowledge, learns to question,
angles for solutions, considers how she's capable.

Exercising as the others sleep, she savours her slow
building of a rampart (translucent, semi-permeable).

Progress

The Glib are loyal customers of Beta. Doctor Love
goes every other day, if not to buy a mouthpiece
or some new accessory for the sex act, then to sit above
the stylish industry of Agerton, shooting the breeze.

At last he drapes Parvit on his arm and takes her there.
(Her expert accommodations have gained results).
She goes disguised, wary of agents, rehearsing stories,
her thoughts turning on procurement of a kinder lease.

No-one can run forever, unless in the sense of asylum.
The city has proved itself a minefield, but she believes
in the power of attention to turn up hidden covens
of largesse in the small, unexplored recesses.

Then there's that other potential, of a different city,
beyond wall and Sky. No-one has spoken of such,
but in her dreams and intuitions there is multiplicity,
a train of opposites; for each flawed unit a haven.

Checkpoint

Traffic slows for sector-crossing at the Krone Circus.
Police patrol the sixteen lanes, randomly checking.

Parvit, also known as 'Lily', has an adequate I.D.,
her picture taken in a new high hairdo. With a

silver-tinted ribbon winding up the black braids, PVC
all-in-one suit, ash-tone skin, she's positively metal.

Simo is her match, long locks bundled in a tight cone.
'Bless you, Lily, you're as hot as a millennium of crush'.

The impresario's *Fuel Cell Supreme* haunts the central hub
like an obsessive thought. New companion each time.

The policeman wants a fraction of this man's finesse,
leans in and grins at the new sally with her turned cheek.

'Mulling at *The Perfect Pill*?' he chummily enquires.
Simo shows his gilded teeth. 'Why break a good habit?'

Who knows how many runaways Febrile has amassed?
Who cares? Eccentric as rain, and just as rich, he can pass.

The Perfect Pill

Psychedelia from moment one. Up in an outdoor lift,
the glass mosaic catching the light like a weaver,
small pictures leaping out, then larger, to confuscation.

Sky-legged, you alight on a deep carpet, colours rising in
3-D; walls carpeted too, with scenes into you could step –
green tunnels with red pouting mouths, ditzy spirals,

eyes in the making of a vortex; pigments in argument,
reaching, pulling apart, compulsive, the screams of them,
their absorption, the inevitable, the neverment, the ever.

She's dissolved and remade, possibles coming crosswise,
no sense but first sense – what she knows only by bone
memory but recognises in shadows and quick glints.

The waiter shows them a host of plants in aeroponic
chambers, roots towards the heat-trapping dome.
'The raw material for our subtle pills, all home grown.
Some are especially powerful in the mix'. He winks.

Doctor Love always sits at the same table.
He holds her hand. She feels the ridges of his rings.
He tells her she's a really special sally. She lifts her chin.

This is Agerton, she tells herself, home of the noble Deft.
If sanctuary exists, it must be here, among the makers.
Crafters augment the world. The rest erode or depend.

Is it sanctuary she wants? Yes, the state of being immune,
as opposed to untouchable. But also the state of activity,
the category of production, a purpose for her limbs.

The meal begins with a procession of plates, an array of
pills, mosaicked to resemble an open eye. She startles.
Don't be paranoid. It's a restaurant, strictly commercial.

Shaken, she finds it hard to gulp or chew, so reverts to
the least resistant – some potent alcohol. *Unwise,*
she reminds herself, lowering the goblet, surprised.

Too many swigs and she might stagger at a crucial step.

INTERPRETATION

They couldn't but ask him to play. Simo Febrile, Maestro.
He saunters to the stage, miming finger-moves, bending
backwards to adore a spirit instrument's upended throat.

He changes the mouthpiece on the bendophone, plays
a scale. A small shake of the head and then he's off,
merged with metal and reed in a chromatic tide.

She's never known him play with such abandon. She
ensieves and yields to him, begins a new osmosis.
All her thoughts shed, she enters an acoustic time

where motive is conferred by tone and timbre.
The floor is hers. The Deft can dance but not like this.
She gives them all she is in rhythm-terms. Here's the city

told in steps, leaps, torso-torts, headswings, its
evolution manifest, the deep mines, the high towers,
marriage, lore, the mystery of Krone, the blind totem.

She stops. A hundred pairs of clapping hands riposte.

Discovered

Parvit is shocked by how concrete she is. She sees herself
in the pupils of other eyes and she is word-worthy.

They say, 'beautiful', 'enchanting', 'eruption', 'fusion',
'crystal-morph' and, most surprising, 'dancer', 'woman'.

The woman walking towards her is thin as a good child,
a tower projecting its virtual (stillness in motion;

windows reflective cells in the business of direction;
pulse not place; the collegiate fabric broaching its truth).

She extends a leaflike hand and slowly Parvit mates it.
It's cool and soft, lace and water; heats at their touch.

'I'm Limber. I want you for my troupe'. The words
are foreign in that arrangement, with that tone of respect.

No answer occurs. Parvit is unversed in choice. Old
habits stir – absence of decision, endless threshold.

Simo re-enters the spotlight. 'Lily does nothing without
me', he says, hand on her shoulder, nails biting.

Diplomacy

Limber's been around the block more than once.
She sinks an expression in the arch of her cheekbones
and leads with an earnest smile in Simo's face.

'Great bendophonists rarely make good dancers',
she croons, 'but you may deliver her on time,
every day at ten, in ballet shoes and a porous leotard.

Though I'd take her in any gear. What a gem you've got'.
He knows he's being played, but it's a sweet enough tune
and her voice is balm to the bristle. He's mollified.

A calyx of pretty nubiles have assembled to adore him.
An irresistible post-show repast. On second thoughts,
the interfering Ballet Dame could be a lucky chance.

'Why don't you two go chat, woman to woman?'
He closes Parvit's fist on a holographic purchase card,
Morph 1. 'The Indolent's Retreat. I'll see you there'.

Parvit goes tableau: a jailbird poised to slip the beam.

At last she has managed a link. She has intertwined self with matrix, as I do. It took music. She took music in and let it turn her insides out, made it the matrix.

Daughter has a sudden thought.

'How large are we?' she asks, immediately realising that the question can only be answered by comparison.

There is silence. Giant has been still for a long time. She might just be turned from Daughter for the present, her attention given to one of her pockets, or to something else. Daughter ponders the possibility of an outside, but not for long. It is essentially imponderable.

'Where did you train? I'm not familiar with your style.
Theta has several good schools. Bella Probis, perhaps?'
Parvit can barely speak. The *Morph 1* etches in her palm.
'I didn't learn. I just got up and ...' 'Got up and dazzled!
You shook the world. Where in god are you from?'
'Aa ... Alpha. Excuse me, I need … the cleansing-room'.
She veers, collides with a table, can't feel her legs.
Could she be losing cohesion, after gaining a frame?
The mirror shows her solid, if blotchy and scare-eyed.
She could creep out a back-window, but she hesitates.
He's generous, and dancing is a form of liberty.
She thinks about the window, can't imagine its beyond.
Instead she treats them to the best *fizz*. Her lies get better.
Both parents dead; her mother a dancer. A kind Null
raised her, and she had little education. Limber gushes.
Breeding shines through. Nature might yet be redeemed.

She goes home with him. She gives him back his card.
He needs to rest. She comforts him. He smells of them.
She lies beside him. Strokes his shoulder. He's fleshy.
She thinks about his bones. Her fingers dowse his chest.
She thanks him for the day. And for the card. And bed.
She skirts the question. It pirouettes. Dusts their lips.
Lily is calm. *Par* is in agitation. Simo falls asleep.
She wakes when he does. She's hardly slept. It's time.
He's on his back. He turns to his side. He'll sleep again.
She palpitates. She pictures the day. It's a dim view.
There is risk. She doesn't know. She must attempt.
Shapes the lips. 'Can Stoker drive me?' He inhales.
He rumbles. He's full of thicken-pills. Staled by brew.
She waits. He grunts. She whispers. 'Alright, then?'
His shoulder shifts. She listens. Traffic on the street.
She slides from bed. Takes her tunic. Dresses as she goes.

ALLY

This time she travels in the boot. Stoker plays dumb.
No-one aims to be a sally. A tire blows, they lose the lane,
tangle with a revolving door. It leads to strange quirks.

All Simo's women have pasts like snapping hounds.
They wear wigs, change scent, assume voices; they're
labyrinths repeated at the centre. But Lily outfogs.

His orders are to watch her, but he'd do that anyhow,
the globe of her rump no more than her fugitive eyes.
Slight woman, stunning event; moves in a glow.

He'll watch her time and cover her tracks. Simo is a fickle
master, but Stoker has information the police might like,
about impregnations among the Stern, a capital crime.

Uncommon activity at the Circus. A thief hopped sector.
The officer has bigger pills to chew than contraband
in the eccentric's *Supreme*. Stoker pledges vigilance. They
nano-urge on; Parvit in the small dark, a child unborn.

Ballon

'In Calgold of Beta, binate towers spiral to their points.
The storeys vary in colour, bespeaking aspiration
to the glorious truths of poly-metamorphic Agelast'.

So goes the *Lore of the Ancestors*. Parvit recalls it as she
stands at the base of Tower no. 9, Calgold, and dizzies
herself with its pleochroic twists. Glorious, she agrees.

All down the street the light is redefined by particular
compositions of the glass. It's said the Deft are closest
in mind to the god, as they never cease creative labour.

She pulls the shining pyrite flap that says 'Ballet Limber'.
The door slides open to narrow corridors, arabesque
icons on the wall, their fingers pointing where.

The eye is host only to its favoured. The sparse room,
the vinyl floor, dancers intent at the barre, the mirrors,
rush at her in a sudden flood, muddling her view.

But the feel of it, in her ears and down low ... *ballon*.

What Her Sinews Won't Do

Isolations. Low bends. Ball-up then splay on all fours.
Right-angled limbs. Lifts and links. Back on back rides.
Flat and upright body crushes. Move in perfect unison.
Floats and slides. Sharp kicks. Meld shape to a tableau.

They won't do it for her, what she's made of. She's back
at the door of her exploded hide, where a tongueless
thought was itself dance, before a lack was named
that swallowed her into a web of discrete perspectives.

Let it go. Give it. A whirl. Stretch. Unwind. Be them.
Let them take the lead, these integrated jewels of nature.
Her muscles refuse, disabled by comparison. *Oh Parvit,*
can you summon no will? Must you be a wallweed?

She's a frozen stream of tears, held in her own season.
The moves are only dreamable and, despite the facts,
it seems she's still asleep, processing shy of the main-
frame; in essence a type of stone, existence her only act.

No Go

Limber has trusted too much, her perennial blunder.
The girl is likely an addict; what else, of the Febrile cote?
She's flat as a leaf and her eyes are like ash-filled pits;
not only does she not comprehend, she can barely stir.

But this body is the same one with skin on fire
that danced its own propellant force and provenance.
Is it the mind that's ruling now? A demon of resistance?
Or maybe one perfect dance was all she had in her.

'Have you never seen a company perform? Yesterday
you skirred through angles and turns. Are you ill?'
(Give her the benefit of the doubt). Not a syllable
through those buttery lips. Limber's patience frays.

'I must see to the others. We have a show. Maybe
come again another day, when you're functional'.
Get lost, she means. Parvit moves to the door, stumbles
over her feet – what a dancer mustn't do (or an escapee).

Daughter-Giant must place Parvit or leave her. This picayune creature with her amorphous desire is neither large enough to be lived in, nor discrete enough to live in something else. She tries to pull back from the sequestered eye. She is neglecting her other locations, and they are in revolt.

UNFAMILIARS

The women talk of spirits in Febrile's red rooms.
Bianca has been roasted by a *pyrgos*.
'I was hot as an oven, I swear.
Three days in bed and in the middle of the third night
I woke, cool for once. Until it rolled through the door.
Not a thing, really – a gathering of heat,
flames flashing from it in a spin, hot arrows.
I could feel my face melting on the bone'.

The others gasp. 'The pain was torture, then terror.
If I was hot before, this was the Age of Fire.
It singed my eyebrows. Look'. Parvit believes.
She herself is in the dark tome of an *izenarg*,
flattened to a dot. She's desiccated by the crush
between its tall adamantine slabs of pages,
their insistent absence of a story, every leaf blank,
all memory of purpose drained to an inkless pen.

SHOT

Mickaela ties a belt on her biceps and inserts the needle.
Her head lolls back, like Simo's in the middle of a tune,
or Grizman's in climax. The muscles of her face turn
traitor. Mechanically, she hands Parvit the works.

Parvit binds the tourniquet and flicks the vein. The air
closes in. She reddens to its hot breath and mute spears.
Simo is doing it with a sally next door, more roughly
than he does with her. This one is just passing through.

Cheerlessly she looks around, at Mickaela's girly walls.
They're only hers while she's kept, but for now she
has put a small stamp on this patch, with her posters
of pop artists and her particular cheap cosmetics.

Parvit is no sally. She does not behave like them.
A queenish poise must be retained, for the memory
of slab-sleep and lone survival. Stickily subconscious,
she sets aside the needle and turns on the TV.

What's On

He's speaking of a curfew to tackle sector violation.
The smallest risk of cleavage must be addressed.
He's confident the citizens will comply.

She trembles at the sight of him, tumult in her chest.
He looks thinner, more tense, eyes rapidly ablink.
Tangy drops tumble into her mouth. She drinks him in.

She recalls the ease of lying in his arms, their harbour,
his mine-deep sobriety and his stillness before a question.
He was wiser. Why did she mock his solemn phrases?

Maybe nothing's better than the first home and hand.
For her they were not the same; one precluded the other.
Home was a hoarse whisper in the ark of compulsion,

the first hand a muzzle clamped to its face. She sees
nothing properly, outside or in. Shapeless again, without
a protective slab, she reaches for the comfort of brew.
If she can't riddle her flesh, she will subdue it.

INTERVENTION

Intent

They know where she is. They'll come for her at night,
while the populace huddles in locked apartments
and a toe's intention sets a long straw of light
sucking on the source, holding it for the drop.

Only indigent cats and reckless criminals venture out
during curfew, though an occasional Deft broaches
the boundaries of skill and consequence by scouting
the streets for blind spots and unsecured niches.

There is one such on the appointed evening. While
the authorities prepare for the grab, she sneaks out
of Mensard, but not for trickery. In emissary style,
her destination is fixed: Dallhog, Theta sector.

She bears the agenda of a secret covey, sworn
to follow the mystical offspring of a megalithic wall.
The blast was revelation. No longer able to contain
its truth, the slate erupted, begging to be heard.

Alva

Alva is taller than the average five micro-urges.
As a girl she stooped to hide the extra half micro,
sat a lot, painted and read, to avoid the brand of freak
on the running track, though she would have done well.

Her skin lacks the gray undertone considered beautiful.
It has a gauzy gleam, like Sky in Her parched breath;
a hint of the same in her hair. *It happens,* she's been told,
but she's also heard whispers calling her a Sky-squirt.

Agelast is all good, but the marriage of Sky and Ground
is uneasy. Jealous of her infinitely fertile mate, Sky
serves down anger with rain, then sears with gelb.
Erratic, it means, *unreliable,* when they call her that.

She's pulled both ways. While the rest mostly look down,
to the organ of resurrection, she also crooks up towards
the sulking canopy, imagining more than she should.
Maybe she was born subversive, listening for the word.

Intruder

All the lifts are monitored, so Alva takes the stairs.
She's been in training since the *Treasure* disappeared,
but still needs to rest every third floor. Some thought
an athlete should be sent, but for once her weirdness
was her trump card. One Sky-squirt to another.

She wonders if the *Treasure* flattens the men of Dallhog,
like Cugele, the spirit consort, who gives ecstatic cover
to every male she meets. Why else shelter in a pleasure-
tower, where sounds of mating pump the air on
every floor, and cloying smells ghost the landings?

The penthouse is a suite with a surround-lounge.
Floor-to-ceiling windows bring the city close.
You'd almost walk through the glass and onto air.
Alva creeps in the low light, rounds a corner. What luck!
the *Treasure,* sprawled on a lavish sofa, head aflop.

Ruddier. Fleshier. And, it seems, partial to glut.

Rescue

'Treasure! Par!' The voice emerges from a lake of static.
An eager face presses towards her. A new sally?
'You must go. They've traced you. They'll soon be here.
I'm one of The Fancy of Par, a small, devoted group.
You are our hope and heroine, a sign of immanent seism.
We call you *Treasure*. You are the apocalyptic gem.
We've been purifying, opening our hearts, staying
free of enhancol, fighting the fear of truth. We pray to
Krone's reflection; what points beneath, inverts above'.

Parvit can't comprehend. She's never hoped or believed.
These are alien concepts. And she, treasure? Ridiculous.
But the other news hauls her to her feet.
'Where will we go?' Alva straightens like a soldier.
'Beta Sector, Mensard, an apartment buried under slabs.
You might feel at home. It's out of the public stare'.
She has nothing to pack. Her body is sufficient gear.

Daughter-Giant shivers, surprising herself. Tides yes, convulsions yes, but a feeling of cold? A gap? Impossible. Despite her efforts, she cannot haul herself or her eye away from Parvit in the cube. Why she has become trapped like this is a mystery to her. It's not as if seeing were her only channel of information. She feel-knows with all of herself, senses dimension and pulse, learns colour from sound, pattern from smell. She is too diverse to be packed into one small viewing box.

'Mother, I must refocus and tend to my other selves. For all I know, Parvit may not be a self at all. Mother?'

There it is again, a swirl of cold. She has always discerned the nature of her mother from her pressing and heaving. By these movements she has known her various states, her areas of power and weakness. Time and space are all the one. She knows what's next and around by the long currents in her own substance. She is both fish and sea, anticipating the onset of a current and being the body of the current herself.

So she knows ... But what she tells herself is another matter.

They suspect he warned her. But he does look dismayed.
He's also angry, rakes the penthouse, smashes things.
He's Simo's first incorruptible bureaucrat and scares him.
Women dash from the rooms or stand back to the walls,
hoping to be liked, maybe taken as mates by the officers.
It won't happen. The sofa is warm, so she couldn't be far.
It's curfew. Only invisible could she avoid detection.
Cameras everywhere, eyes in the slate, all units alert.

But they don't know the Fancy's tunnel under the wall.
The *Treasure* and her acolyte are already there, crawling
towards upper-left corner. It's familiar ground, but
there's still terror of a cave-in. Brew-beset Parvit
hunts for pretty pictures, finds: a blue-and-white globe;
a long-legged insect; bubbles in a limpid glass; lush
leaves; glossy lipstick; a yellow ball in a blue over-sky.
Memory becomes flesh and she totally recalls.

In a second tunnel, the women feel for a sense of space.
It's long in coming. Parvit recalls her bout of discipline
and breathes slowly. Present darkness and illumined past
intersect, converse to the cramped ambit of limbs.
Her mind flees the scene, delves into its new memories,
verifies each episode, makes it vivid as a brand.
A whole new scenario, and she the single open eye.

The torch on Alva's head lights a rough stairs. Trembling,
sweat mating with tears, they haul themselves up
the crooked steps. Alva knocks. The trapdoor is lifted.
They arrive in a small room, gasping, limp as wet sheets.
A chant begins, incense is lit, small bells struck.
They are draped in slim cloaks of gray and white.
Parvit remembers hard floors and convulsively weeps.
It is warm, perhaps safe, but she must suffer the burden
of her new truth, her body the axis of a cosmic heresy.

GURU

Here her devotees, eyes pregnant with her, offering food.
Simple fare on a filigreed dish ornate with gems.
It's how they understand godliness. What if she said
she desires bubble-filled wine, sugar-dusted cream cakes,
juicy meats, and, generally, to be chock-full oblivious?
She only has memories of these, and papillose reactions
impossible to chart, that crop up like random lights.
She might dance it, if her body could forgive its failures.
Treasure. Godborn. The words impale her like a pinioned
lepidopteron, potential trapped in a phrase.
The foisted tasks are huge. *Save them from necessity.*
Lead them out of themselves. Push back the slate horizon
and peel off Sky. They might even expect to survive.
The only possible line of flight is the gelben capillary,
and how harness that? 'Take me back to my first niche',
she says. 'I think my soul is still there, beating the walls'.

Power Play

Ben is the brains of The Fancy. His stony eyes claim her,
appraising how well she fits the sibylline role, and how
to preserve his influence in the light of her presence.

'You'll be pleased to hear', he ventures, 'that we've
opened a tunnel to your grotto. We venerate it. You'll
find it bedecked with lanterns, beads and votive notes'.

She blenches. Her organs huddle inward, cringing.
She works to stay composed. 'It's been some time'.
He doesn't answer. Reassurance is not his style.

'They've rebuilt the wall', says Alva, 'which suits us'.
She grins. 'Most citizens have forgotten where it was.
No-one speculates in Archonbase. They trust their eyes'.

It will be another crouch in the solid dark, with Ben's
canny breathing at her neck, his constant, silent analysis.
The others are credulous, needy for love, but Ben is a
power-player. She has no divine missile to unsettle him.

Limbo

All that's precious is said to reside deep within Ground,
hidden in the murk until the right blast resurrects it.
Is Parvit a living gem, first child of a new progeniture?
If so, why is she mutinous, even while she sleeps?
She barely resembles a citizen, with her lustrous skin,
hair the colour of carrots and a body like walking water.
If her origin is elsewhere, how did she lodge so deep?

They crawl silently towards her sill. She's ashamed of it.
Resentful too, that it's no longer her sole sanctum.
Not that it's a home, but it's a place her mind can muster
when all knowledge fails, where she dwelled as a right.
Ben makes a platform of his hands and lifts her up.
The slate has solid warmth, like soapstone after fire.
She huddles, feels for the signal wisdom of dwellings.

No nostalgia. Only a blank, gray discomfort. This was
never more than a passageway. She was born to leave.

Arrest

She's in the air above the stone and is she boneless again?
It feels like mother gelb reaching in to snatch her darling.
Take me, spew me out upon your great, allcoloured world.

For a tumid moment she's afloat, amid a glaring light.
Then she falls, in rock-hail and scatterings of dust.
She slips into stillness. If this is death, it's welcome.

Resurrection. Machinic shifting. Military voices.
'Did you think you could deceive Agelast? Burrow all
you like, you're still in the body of all-knowing god'.

She stares at the stone above and decides there is no such
soft thing as a soul. The body can't revert to its crucible.
She hears his offered hand, knows his eyes are suffering.

She won't meet them. He helps her down, guides her
over the shattered slate to an armoured van. It dawns
on her that no-one can aspire to freedom.
There's only surrender to a force, outer or inner.

INTERROGATION

THE BODY CAGE

They are side by side in the van, rain pelting the roof.
Habit clues her to his hidden stirrings, and his bonds.
She wants him unzipped, his legislating bulk upon her.
She sits on sweat and ooze. An equal force forbids her
to unroll the tight ball inside and dissolve it in action.

She won't return his gestures, silently recites a string
of grievances: his lack of talk; his presumption of right;
his inability to place himself inside her skin except to
stretch it; his failure to manage her. He was her first
shaper and cast her in a bad mould, taught her shame.

She finds him watching. His eyes dilate and recollect.
She won't admit it. She has been doubly betrayed.
He'd reduce her to generic capability. All that admiration
was foisted apotheosis. Same as The Fancy of Par, who'd
see her frozen in one position so they could mount her.

Her muscles tighten. Out of oblivion, into the body cage.

Oblivion and body are not in Daughter's experience, but she is keenly feeling caged. Locked to her eye, locked in the cube, locked to Parvit, she is losing her immense mobility. Instead she is being worked on and rearranged, traversed by a multitude of thin, cold streams she can't feel as her own.

'I am too long here', she wails. 'I will lose what I am'.

She becomes a deep lament, knowing there will be no answer. But as the streams continue, it becomes clear they are not slicing her; they are making her swell. They are merging with her substance and adding new attributes. She is augmented in all her lives, an altogether more considerable selfdom.

'Oh, Mother!' she exclaims.

Inside the Krone

They enter slowly through Funeral Gate. On for
several minutes, then the van circles, judders to still.
The ranting sound of metal. A pervasive, resonant hum.
'I love you', he whispers. 'Remember that. Please'.

She pictures the four letters as sectors, initialising:
Lean Over Very Erotically (please). She will not.
Or she will. To elude them again. To subvert them.
Is she a fighter, so? Where has survival ever taken her?

Eight silent policemen form an escort, Grizman leading.
Traitor. To kiss and turn her over to the blind totem.
They cross the large hall, skirting hearses and trolleys,
rows of shrouded burdens. What is this, a corpse glut?

Ascending in the lift, her skin registers pore-spiking heat.
The men stare blankly at the steel doors, as if compliance
were the only way, action a pre-ordained thing. They will
mould or melt her, she thinks, and is she a treasure?

The Central Chamber

Here is the hum, a sustained low intoning by the priests.
They face the wall; the chant is caught by the pyramid
and conflated to an echo chamber. A sonic ouroboros,

occupying every head like a flood of ink. Thoughts wade
in the sound, are shredded to long, flaccid leaves and
Parvit knows she's defeated. She will not escape this.

The knowledge brings focus – like the onset of rain,
a sprint up ten flights, or a raw thrust when she's dry.
She gathers herself, her twigs, into one sharp spear.

Kayman, Hierocyclus, Corpse Cook, is at the furnace
in a red sampot, hair tied back, holding X on his chest a
hammer and chisel, framing a tattoo of the closed eye.

Cineron has compass and set square. A scientist, Dorimu,
makes calls. The table is fitted with steel bonds. She will
please them before knives are applied, or weights, or fire.

Grizman stands at the table, hands empty, head down.

On the Table

'We will question you, and for each evasion the steel
bonds will be squeezed more tightly. Understand?'
She can barely nod, her head restrained in a fixed helmet.

'Your blood is Agelastian and your functions normal,
but you lived without food or drink, within godwall,
alone, untended. Explain how you emerged healthy'.

'I can't, but this is what I remember: short lucid periods
when I felt the city, and saw it as one does on a screen. I
scratched pictures on the wall of objects I didn't know.

Mostly I slept, dreaming of a world beyond Sky, where
gelb sometimes took me to liberate the joy in things'.
The triumvirate purse their mouths. The scientist keys.

Parvit trembles, not all from fear; Ground has lurched.
'Please. Unlock me. Where can I go?' Grizman stirs,
but Cineron snaps the callipers. Kayman intones:
'Bane of Agelast, reveal yourself. Show us your source'.

EVASION

Grizman begins to talk. She should know. The corpses,
the heat, the tremors: Ground is caving in and prayers

have brought no answer from the god. 'Anxious citizens
are being calmed by talk of a new, great metamorphosis.

We say that some of our beloved must act as sacred fuel'.
'There is truth in it', Kayman asserts, wary of trespass.

Dorimu interjects. 'Miners died in chamber collapse,
period. Our resources are gone. Autopoiesis is over'.

He's respected, allowed to speak, even when three years
ago he came with a doomsday prediction and a plan.

'It's no consolation to be right. As to speed, I was wrong.
Upper-left subsidence and Sateset's rift took two hours'.

To Parvit: 'What is the other world? Can it sustain life?
What you know may save us'. Sweating, she croaks, 'I'm

not sure how I formed or what I saw. It's all like dream'.
One lucky stroke of gelb, she reckons, *and she's saved.*

Machinations

They're not fools. Kayman tightens the bonds.
A tremor takes his attention, and Cineron barks at her.
'You said you travelled in the body. Which is it?'
'I thought I travelled, but nothing is clear'.

Dorimu muses: 'Either Sky has depth equal to Ground's,
to mine for weather, or it's a thin filter for a source
beyond. Travel is the only way of knowing,
and that's like casting waste over the godwall'.

'Citizens are not waste', Grizman says. Dorimu nods.
He's close to blasphemy, but is confident of his value.
'A young Deft, Sconis, has devised a machine that can
harness gelb and propel upwards a small vehicle'.

Grizman is shocked. 'He has worked on this in secret?
How many others?' Kayman's blandness hints at deceit.
'Are you in favour?' The hierarch lowers his head.
'Who knows what refuge god has built for the faithful?'

SURRENDER

The world is a broken egg. Nothing stands.
What must she say to be redeemed?
The air in the chamber is blistered as a burnt pill.

Grizman sneaks a hand onto her shoulder.
It cools, at point of touch, and deep in her belly.
But it reminds her of their bed and brands her traitor.

Gelben. Indiscriminate wrecker of harmony. Disloyal.
Worm. Small-minded. Caring for no-body but herself,
not even for the one who made living most beautiful.

She cries. Sharp tears for all the hidden histories,
people with noble aims she parodied or shunned.
Such trivial concerns she had, and now there is death.

'I should have slept', she sobs, almost choking. 'I am a
blasphemous desiring eye. *The gaze must cling to what is*
solid, never stray'. Cineron gasps. 'She quotes The Lore!'
(*Behold the captured renegade, baring her throat*).

Denuded

'You are the False One?' *The One. The Unamalgamated.*
Ground and Sky align, enmity forgotten, hatchet against

her. She's an army of one, that is no army; what army
is armless, legless, eyeless, except one whored by history?

Pain is only guest until drunk; then it's edacious host,
turns ravenous and beastish. Gullet universal, it renders

indistinguishable each tang and spice from bone, until
chyme is atmosquare, every bite munched to its least.

Bubble-current. Sunken. Memory bit. Gray's dull shade.
Contracted without benefit. Screams expressing nothing,

no relief but in mutation, no, in abandonment, but who
knows what continues when one ceases to look?
Conquered, she closes.

Stunned, the men watch her body suck itself in. The face
fades, the limbs deflate and recede. She is fireclay.

Grizman collapses like a falling tent on her lifeless
not-her body. Torture, to hold only the unshapely source.

The cube around Daughter-eye trembles and the eye flattens a little, as if about to melt. Daughter opens a pocket in herself.

'Come', she says, 'there is time and space'.

And then she wonders to whom she speaks, because couldn't she embrace them all?

'She *is* something other! Gelb-come, how else!'
'Debatable. There's no proof of anything beyond Sky.
Gelb is electricity, powerful if harnessed, but as
air travel untried'.
            'Still you would risk it?'
                                    'Rather than extinction'. Dorimu
fingers his phone: 'We must analyse the body'.

Kayman and Cineron consult, as Grizman openly sobs.
Pernicious, her hold on him. Contaminating, weakening.
There is tacit agreement. One, definite, to be left behind.

Dorimu lowers the phone, rigid with shock. 'Rupture
in Gamma. Archonbase is crumbling. The faults are
at both ends of the diagonal. The centre will be next'.
He beckons. 'Put her on a bier and cover her. Bring the
armoured vehicles. Mensard Laboratory, without delay'.

'Hold', Kayman cries. 'She has intimated guilt, so she
must be burnt. It may propitiate the god'. Dorimu gulps.
In matters of divine intention, the hierarch trumps.

Parvit Dreams her Redemption

It is her face at the window of a high tower. At her back,
tormenters prime their instruments and plans. *We'll strip*
you down, Little Miss, you'll like that. We'll search you

everywhere for the hardened spot, the rogue nipple
of Sky-squirts. Where do you hide your litter? Pink
abominations in your murky crevice, hard and hot.

By Agelast, you'll sit on the stool with your legs tethered
and we'll see then, we'll see what comes to your comfort.
You'll be weeping and gibbering to their flighty noggins.

We'll sliver you. We'll walk you till you blister, then
sit you on a point sharper than gelb-stick. We'll burn your
skin and make your outside ugly as your inner.

She projects an athame, carves from the air a circle
that is globe, the spirit *rigatus*, warm protecting vessel,
all window, her face within, revolving. The tower
buckles, not from gelb, but from this wizard thought.

Four priests roll a bier to the table and wait. If this were
a normal corpse, they'd drape it in the consecrated cloth
and offer prayers to ease its transit into the ambient god.
Cloth strips would be slid under, by degrees, rods
at the ends for grip. The body would be shifted to the
bier and sacred ash cast, for the sake of igneous time.

But these remains are surely spiritless. No dead animal
is blessed and she is much lower – formless, abominable.
'We must preserve her', Dorimu repeats. Cineron shakes
his head. 'She was born at crisis; died at crisis. If she
is organic to adversity, even her corpse is a traitor'.

Grizman straightens up. 'If this is a Council matter, I
agree to her sacrifice, but by crush and implosion,
on her first stone bed; I to carry it out, if it please god'.
He wraps her, gathers her up, proceeds to the lift.
Dorimu looks to the others for a word. There is none.

BREAKING POINT

but a welter a thousand thick surrounds the dawn Krone.
They come from all quarters, regardless of their bodies'
inequivalence to the Slate Father. Rain won't spare them,
but neither will He. Two reservoirs have sprung cracks
and in a while the city may resemble prehistoric lake.
Can they imagine it? And the inviolable walls tumbled?
The gates of the Krone are lifted; policemen brace shields.
Exit the priests under canopy, girded by chant and
incense, the vessel of the Closed Eye borne by Kayman.
The idol is awesome and is rarely shown, but the crowd
doesn't draw back. There's a clash of currents in it,
like soup being stirred several ways. When the armoured
cars appear, and the government vehicles, a desperate
roar, of ancient insecurities and doubt, gathers all voices
in a raucous, blood-lit challenge. Abruptly, rain ceases.
In that instant, the convoy escapes. Grizman also, loaded.

Larval

He has carried her before. Over thresholds. Upstairs.
She was never a load for him, the stalwart.

Now she hardly has mass at all, a small parcel. But icy.
Neither haste nor the prevailing panic warms him.

He's shocked by the new Archonbase, its leering rift,
gaps for towers. It has vomited itself in messy shards.

Sky is bright when they reach the wall. The inner layer
has toppled, but the stone bed remains, marmoreally wet.

He places her, pulls himself after, in tremors. Nothing
sensate could rest here. Was she so intimate with slate?

Unless he can retract his senses, he can't be her die-hard.
He might gain her metabolic sloth by concentration. She's

rubbery, but something solid must be clenched inside,
a collapsed skeleton. He presses her random lumps.

She may be elemental, her embodiment a once-off.
He strips, curls to her back, croons, 'Now. Together'.

STREET DIALECTIC

– It is her, pray to her. Love her and she'll redeem you.
She of the hidden cleft, the cloven slate, Ground held foetal
until the hour of the New Order. Follow her and you will live.

– Blasphemers! Ground rejected her. She is destruction,
the false vein, the weak trend, the lamina that breaks.
She must be hunted and crushed for the greater number.

– Her birth was a sign. She came to the visions of the initiate.
Ground loves her and will not relent until you embrace her.
She is His Treasure, His Great Daughter, the One True Gem.

– Excrescence on the godface. Erosion of life's build.
Blaster of towers. Rotting cut stem. Sky-scum.
They say she rode the gelb. A policeman heard her tell it.

– Believe! Open your hearts! She is merger, not dissolution.
Womb-tear of the greater god, healer of the Ground-Sky rift.
She will bring us into the Template, eyes open, fully alive.

– Burn the desecrating eyes! Shoot their ashes to the void.

PARVIT'S OWN GRID

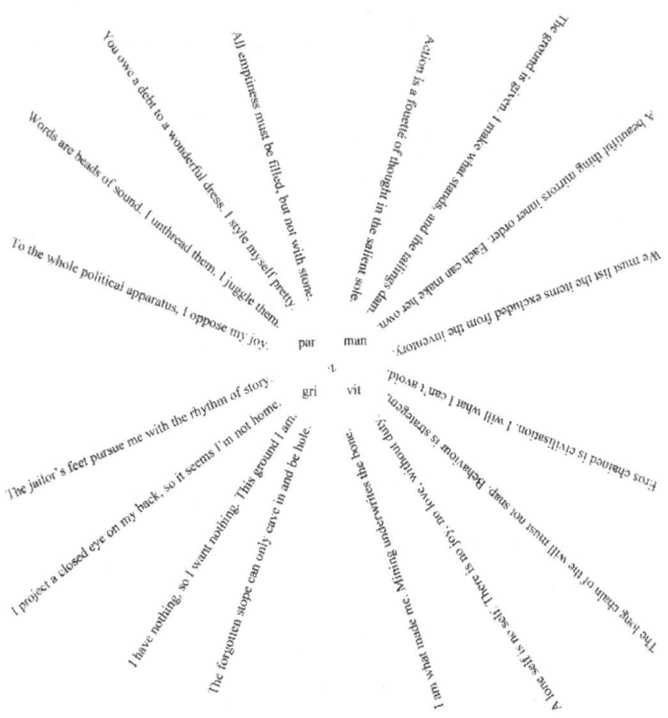

So, I am alone, Giant tells herself, finally accepting her Mother's dissolution. *I am the instigator now.*
How long has she watched Agelast and its disaffect? Does it matter? She is calm, taut in all her parts, ready for action. Like Parvit, she has also wanted to wander pointlessly and let some other consciousness manage the world for her. She has not known how to act with focus, only to scurry about from one location to another. But are not all those locations within herself? *I am the world.* The only thing outside is the interstitial space that eludes her awareness.

Mob

They all feel the heating of the air. It's an inner agitation,
curries the paler of them, roseates the gray to the quick.
They're ablaze with doing the necessary, except

they have no concept of anything, just the rabid clicks
in their physical apparatus. Stop, go, flow, stick –
whatever seems most akin to the self-preservative.

They surround the unfortunate prison van. They tip it
over on its side. Small people, but built like bricks.
This hot number could knock a dent in a monolith

tall as a tower. Everything's coming down in a tick
anyway, so pulverise the blasphemers if you can't hit
on any other reason. Haul 'em from the van and kick

'em down the street to the Krone – or no, to her hitching
hole. Nullify 'em there, in that mephitic little niche.
Pass the torches, sport 'em. Mind your hair. Trick

is, keep 'em high. Save your swing for the crucial pitch.

PRIMED

Expert in the chemical shifts induced by gelb, Sconis
notes its particular features in the present change of air.
His propulsion machine is on the roof above the Lab
in a custom-built hangar. His team adjust and repair.

The concept was simple, the execution an act of genius.
Several years of random experiments, then support
enough to build a structure and begin concerted tests.
Only this month was it ready for the first (or final) junket

– fortuitous timing, with the rapid collapse of the mines.
A trial run and the launch of a data-collector would have
been ideal. All that's known of Sky is gelb and rain.
What other complex matter might it hold in its enclaves?

The sensors confirm that gelb is not just imminent but all-
pervasive. The scientists watch the yellow heat melding
with air and scramble to predict its course. Sconis calls
an elite few to the roof, where all is primed for blasting.

Dorimu brings fifteen others: Kayman half in trance;
Cineron shuddering; two police chiefs for muscle;
two engineers; eight women (none of them wives),
nubile, for mating. Dorimu has been pragmatic here,
has himself left a cherished wife and child. As for
the scientists of Mensard, only Sconis will go.

In a way they've been prepared. On Kroneday citizens
recite: *All dues to Allfather and respect to Allmother Sky.*
To the one we give our dark focus, to the other our averted eyes.
There is nothing but the god, and in it all that is, resides.
In it, of it, with it, to preserve and serve it, we live and die.

Sconis announces almost full gelben power. Goodbyes
are brief. The chosen payload climb to the machine,
wearing white over-suits and masks against projected
dangers. Seals and systems are checked, roof rolled back
to the engorged target. All poised, for ignition or furnace.

Blast Off

The mob drives on, moving joints in the mounting heat
of a great oven, stumbling over the fallen, towards
Parvit's vault. Some dart into unstable towers, as Ground
rumbles. There's the feel of a kettle approaching screech.

Who is gelb? But it's there, building to a grand entrance.
The scalding vapour hardens to a claw, then spikes, as if
shooting through a porous cap. Instantly, Theta's
water tower breaks with a great reverberating roar.

Sight and sound one all-consuming flash. The lucid few
rush for cover, the others shrivel. Bodies become paving
stones, pressed, griddle-baked. Agelast is a shriek,
caving and spewing, ancient godwall dislodging.

The Levecott wall goes like a domino, is swallowed by
water gush, pitted against its element. No revelation.
No-one can look. If they could, whether dying or bolting,
they would see the flaming tail of a metal bird, flown.

No day or night, no Sky, Ground, dimension or direction.
All that defines the state of being is a shard multiplying
in a long series: black, yellow, red. A popping clone pot,
boiled up by something unavailable, some impossible
mathematics a million imprecations will not dint.

Where it started, questions at all, lie buried in this
first final state without shape or numerical division.
Zero would be mercy. This is absence of ground, *nought*
voracious, all numbers baked in it and what they make
is meat for a mouth no creature owns, maw so wide
it is the only body, fat with the greed of universal gape.

They crouch in the tiny spaces between deaths and find
they are crushed. Names and promises are broken down
by some necessity. The Krone sinks. The reservoir
in Gamma bursts. Time's passage derails into a vortex,
inscrutable flux of fire and water; a scorch-edged yawn.

Loyal

Some wristwatches work, so old time can be construed,
but shock and oblivion may have stolen some days.
It's no advantage to tread a notional hour when you're
cramped under a slab, waiting for abatement.
Unless, like some Deft, you have the nerve to listen
for a mode in the mayhem and try predicting its course.
It's clear to this few that something took the water off.
Has Ground sunk a great funnel, maybe at the Krone?
By slow thought, a stranger theory emerges: the collapse
of the city wall – as hard to believe as a debunked god.
Ben and Alva believe, hunting havens under Gamma,
standing waist-high in water, gauging every sound.
They last sixteen days.

Parvit sleeps on. Grizman doesn't trouble to survive.
When the reservoir tide carries them, he sees her dry on a
mound and ebbs with the fluent god in his lungs, unable
to swim, and with his last, burdened breath, still loyal.

Perhaps I do not encompass everything, Giant thinks. If I cannot change the course of what I see, then it might be coming from outside. I only know what I focus on, and I can rarely intervene.

The thought stuns her. What has all her movement been for? What has been her purpose? Her matrix suddenly seems an ocean of ignorance.

She is only thinly held to the eye by now, but she is still bound, and attempts at focusing elsewhere don't succeed. In effect, she is unfocused. Although she sees the events onscreen, she is no longer involved.

NOMAD

After

She wakes with long limbs and sharp vision,
broad-shouldered, flexible.
She is on a height and can see a long distance.
Above is a vaulted, motile sky, blue and white,
a disinterested sun.
She casts a shadow and knows herself by it.

In one direction, an immense dark sierra
of shattered slate and metal waste.
Light flounders there, loses its volitant body,
dwindles to a thinly spread sheen.
There is no sense of a beyond.
Only faith might construe a farther world.

The other way, light is happier.
It finds reflection in industry and free migration.
She recognises the scurry of gainful lives,
the troglodytes beneath the beam.
Workers are processing waste and remoulding it.
It is the stuff of their dwellings.

She picks her way down the hill of shattered stone,
the discards of mining.
There are people at the base, beginning to work this too.
They are welcoming. They give her
something more than a gray cloth to wear
as she walks towards the ruins.

She is lost in recollection:
a hand leaving food on a dim ledge;
a face seeping into hers, making itself a mask;
a body spooned to her back.
The visions propel her, unaware of her progress,
until the sun is well past zenith and she steps on slate.

SURVIVORS

It's a kind of path and she follows it.
It takes her a snaky route between close accidental walls.
There are torn garments and the odd vessel or utensil,
but no hint of movement.
Where will she rest?
Nightfall here will be total.

She gathers what soft cloth she finds.
She might at least make a mattress.
Some of the fabric has the warm feel of life,
so it has not been long since the collapse.
She wants to pick up everything and
see what she can make with potsherds

and stray gems. In the morning
she'll devise a kind of grid and work her way
through the ruins in a salvage operation.
There may be trapped survivors.
She has no idea how she will rescue them,
but she's inclined to endeavour.

She rounds a corner into a large space
containing the wreck of a pyramid.
There are makeshift slate huts and a group
of children round a fire, clumsily roasting a pig.
One of them runs to her.
'Are you the Treasure? There's a letter from Ben'.

He peers. 'Your hair is a little orange, yes, but you're tall,
and your eyes are slate-gray, not whitish blue'.
'I am the Treasure', she says.
'I lived in this city. The letter is for me'.
She reads it in the twilight,
two bereaved children snuggled at her breasts.

BEN'S LETTER TO PARVIT

Parvit,
So, you've re-embodied and there are survivors.
So much is victory. This letter is to tell you your origin.
Fifty years ago, a scientist called Minbar found a small
efflorescence in a disused mine chamber.
Its consistency was of cooked egg and flesh.
He took it to his lab and found it had a pulse.

He kept it secret in his home, tried to simulate its
environment, watched how it behaved. It grew
an exoskeleton, responsive to stimuli. He began a
'schooling', applied information in various ways. Though
with no organ of sense, it could learn by absorption.

It consumed small pills, but in time weakened; revived
in a niche within godwall, but ingested its outer bone.
After Minbar, my father took up watch, then I. I applied
mutations and you emerged. So be assured: you are true
progeny of Ground. Grizman must have sensed it.

I am also your father in a way, so, as god is silent,
let me pass on your present mission: Rebuild.
Agelast forever.
Yours.

Nostos

She begins to sing. For the children. For nothing.
Of things
none of them knows –
fields of buttercups and corn, mountain rivers,
braces of fish, endless seas,
colonies founded on the verge of cities.
Of the colours that announce darkness
and the two crows eyeing the carcass of dinner.
The children run from them. They are slate-coloured,
unlike the known birds, who are white,
low-flying, docile.
The crows feast like natives,
hooded as the children themselves,
and take to the air.
All eyes follow them into the vivid sunset.
And retract. And close.
'No', she says, 'you may look'.
So they look and are not hurt.
They watch until Sky
becomes a cloth studded with gems.
'Is it gelb?' they whisper.
'They are Sky's mines, signalling to us'.
Their hoods fall back and someone starts to laugh,
in the tone of star-silver.
They all do, then fall silent, shocked.
'There is time', she tells them.
'You will look and laugh'.
She studies the patterns in the stars
as the children give in to sleep.
Tomorrow she will lead them towards the satellite towns.
'Where will we live?' a Deft boy asks,
scrunching his eyelids.
'In our city. And out of it. We are all Treasure'.
He doesn't understand, but it is an answer.
A flashing light moves across the sky
like a shuttle through a concourse.

Are they still travelling?
The vessel measures its pace among the stars,
        circling as if bound.
How will I be if it never disappears? she asks herself.
She finds that she is seeping blood
and forgets the question.

The eye closes. The cube and screen collapse. Giant breathes in. For a while she lives in that breath as in a void, feel-knowing nothing. When she comes to awareness again, she finds a separate, smaller presence restless against her.

Daughter, she says. *Go run.*

ABOUT THE AUTHOR

Máighréad Medbh was born in County Limerick, where she grew up in semi-isolation, and currently maintains her bewildered existence in Swords, Co. Dublin. She has published six poetry collections, and has become widely known as a performance poet since the publication of her first book. More recently, she has written three novels, online as ebooks, and a serialised story for children for Ireland's Lyric FM. In 2013, Dedalus Press published *Savage Solitude: Reflections of a Reluctant Loner,* an exploration of the fear of loneliness through reading and dramatised response. Her work has been translated into Galician and German, and appears in many Irish and international anthologies, as well as several academic works. With a liking for exploring themes, Máighréad has written a narrative sequence on the famine, and one based on astrology. In 2015, she collaborated with the artist, Bernie Masterson, in the making of an art film. She was 2016 winner of the Listowel Writers' Week Single Poem competition. Subscribe to her monthly blog on www.maighreadmedbh.ie

Máighréad's poetry collections are:
Pagan to the Core (Arlen House, 2014)
Twelve Beds for the Dreamer (Arlen House, 2010)
When the Air Inhales You (Arlen House, 2008)
Split in *¡Divas!* (Arlen House, 2003)
Tenant (Salmon Publishing, 1999)
The Making of a Pagan (Blackstaff Press, 1990)

'net' was previously published in *And Agamemnon Dead: An Anthology of Early Twenty First Century Irish Poetry*, eds. Peter O'Neill & Walter Ruhlmann (Paris, Muavaise Graine, 2015).
'Smalled' was published in *The Stony Thursday Book,* No. 13, Autumn 2014, ed. Peter Sirr.
'cut' was published in *The Stinging Fly*, Issue 27, Volume Two, Spring 2014.